RULES OF THUMB

A GUIDE FOR WRITERS

Fifth Edition

Good Measures: A Practice Book to Accompany Rules of Thumb

(Exercises keyed to the pages of *Rules of Thumb*)

Rules of Thumb for Business Writers

Rules of Thumb for Research

Rules of Thumb for Online Research

(by Diana Roberts Wienbroer)

Writing from the Inner Self

(by Elaine Hughes)

RULES OF THUMB

A GUIDE FOR WRITERS

Fifth Edition

JAY SILVERMAN
Nassau Community College

ELAINE HUGHES
Nassau Community College

DIANA ROBERTS WIENBROER
Nassau Community College

Boston   Burr Ridge, IL   Dubuque, IA   Madison, WI   New York
San Francisco   St. Louis   Bangkok   Bogotá   Caracas   Kuala Lumpur
Lisbon   London   Madrid   Mexico City   Milan   Montreal   New Delhi
Santiago   Seoul   Singapore   Sydney   Taipei   Toronto

McGraw-Hill Higher Education

A Division of The McGraw-Hill Companies

RULES OF THUMB: A GUIDE FOR WRITERS

Published by McGraw-Hill, an imprint of The McGraw-Hill Companies, Inc. 1221 Avenue of the Americas, New York, NY, 10020. Copyright © 2002, 2000, 1999, 1996, 1993, 1990 by Jay Silverman, Elaine Hughes, and Diana Roberts Wienbroer. All rights reserved. No part of this publication may be reproduced or distributed in any form or by any means, or stored in a data base or retrieval system, without the prior written consent of Jay Silverman, Elaine Hughes, and Diana Roberts Wienbroer, including, but not limited to, in any network or other electronic storage or transmission, or broadcast for distance learning. Some ancillaries, including electronic and print components, may not be available to customers outside the United States.

This book is printed on acid-free paper.

2 3 4 5 6 7 8 9 0 DOC/DOC 0 9 8 7 6 5 4 3 2

ISBN 0-07-283660-1

Editorial director: *Phillip A. Butcher*
Executive editor: *Lisa Moore*
Editorial coordinator: *Victoria Fullard*
Senior marketing manager: *David Patterson*
Project manager: *Rebecca Nordbrock*
Production supervisor: *Susanne Riedell*
Producer, media technology: *Todd Vaccaro*
Freelance design coordinator: *Gino Cieslik*
Supplement associate: *Kate Boylan*
Cover design: *Carla Pacilio*
Typeface: *11/13 Palatino*
Compositor: *Shepherd Incorporated*
Printer: *R. R. Donnelley & Sons Company*

Library of Congress Cataloging-in-Publication Data

Silverman, Jay, 1947-
   Rules of thumb : a guide for writers / Jay Silverman, Elaine Hughes, Diana Roberts Wienbroer.—5th ed.
     p. cm.
   Includes index.
   ISBN 0-07-283660-1 (acid free paper)
   1. English language—Rhetoric—Handbooks, manuals, etc. 2. English language—Grammar—Handbooks, manuals, etc. 3. Report writing—Handbooks, manuals, etc. I. Hughes, Elaine. II. Wienbroer, Diana Roberts. III. Title
PE1408. S4878 2002
808.'042—dc21

2001037002

www.mhhe.com

CONTENTS

PART 1: CORRECTNESS

PART 2: PUTTING A PAPER TOGETHER

PART 3: THE RESEARCH PAPER

PART 4: GROWING AS A WRITER

ACKNOWLEDGMENTS

For their careful reading and questioning of various drafts of *Rules of Thumb,* we wish to thank Beverly Jensen; Polly Marshall, Hinds Community College; Nell Ann Pickett, Hinds Community College; and Larry Richman, Virginia Highlands Community College. Special thanks go to Sue Pohja, of Langenscheidt Publishers, Inc., whose enthusiasm for this book helped to create a trade edition. Lisa Moore, our editor at McGraw-Hill, has given *Rules of Thumb* a new burst of life by appreciating its virtues but also encouraging us to think about it in new ways.

We especially want to thank Ethel and Jimmy Pickens, Peggy Griffin, Ruth Green, and Peggy Sue Dickinson for all sorts of logistical help, and even more for their love and their spirit.

We are grateful for the encouragement and enthusiasm of our colleagues in the English Department at Nassau Community College. In particular, we wish to thank Paula Beck, James Blake, Mimi Quen Cheiken, Kathryn Tripp Feldman, Rebecca Fraser, Emily Hegarty, Jeanne Hunter, Bernice Kliman, Hedda Marcus, Kathy McHale, John Tucker, Dominick Yezzo, and Scott Zaluda. Jeffrey Wohler, a student, asked valuable questions that improved this edition.

We also appreciate the thoughtful comments of Jeffrey Andelora, Arizona State University; Andrew J. Auge, Loras College; Janet Auten, American University; Doris Barkin, City College; Judy Bechtel, North Kentucky University; Joyce Bender, Oklahoma Panhandle State University; Michel de Benedictis, Miami Dade Community College; Chris Brooks, Wichita State University; Michael Browner, Miami Dade Community College; Tim Bywater, Dixie College; Joseph T. Calabrese, University of Nevada; Robin Calitri, Merced College; Lawrence Carlson, Orange Coast College;

Diana Cox, Amarillo College; Katherine Restaino Dick; Ralph G. Dille, University of Southern Colorado; Michael DiRaimo, Manchester Community College; Steffeny Fazzio, Salt Lake Community College; Susan Finlayson, Adirondack Community College; Ellen Gardiner, University of Mississippi; James F. Gerlach, Northwestern Michigan College; Matthew Goldie, NYCTC; Robert Hach, Miami-Dade Community College; Andrew Halford, Paducah Community College; Marie Iglesias-Cardinale, Genesee Community College; Jacqueline Lautin, Hunter College; Mary McFarland, Fresno City College; Kurt Neumann, William Rainey Harper College; David Norlin, Bethany College; Roger Ochse, Black Hills University; Patricia Harkins Pierre, University of the Virgin Islands; Bonnie Plumber, Eastern Kentucky University; Sims Cheek Poindexter, Central Carolina Community College; Retta Porter, Hinds Community College; Bruce Reeves, Diablo Valley College; Lois Ann Ryan, Manchester Community Technical College; Sara L. Sanders, Coastal Community College; Jeanne Smith, Oglala Lakota College; Stephen Straight, Manchester Community College; and A. Gordon Van Ness III, Longwood College; Winnie Wood, Wellesley College; Mary Zdrojkowski, University of Michigan.

This book would not have existed but for our students—both as the audience we had in mind and as perceptive readers and critics.

Jay Silverman
Elaine Hughes
Diana Roberts Wienbroer

How to Use *Rules of Thumb*

This book is for you if you love to write, but it's also for you if you *have* to write. *Rules of Thumb* is a quick guide that you can use easily, on your own, and feel confident in your writing.

We suggest that you read *Rules of Thumb* in small doses, out of order, when you need it. It's not like a novel that keeps you up late into the night. You'll need to read a few lines and then pause to see if you understand. After ten minutes, set the book aside. From time to time, look at the same points again as a reminder.

> Part 1, "Correctness," covers the most common mistakes. We put these rules first because they are what most students worry about and will want to have handy. However, when you are writing your ideas, don't get distracted with correctness; afterwards, take the time to look up the rules you need.

> Part 2, "Putting a Paper Together," takes you through the stages of writing an essay—from coming up with ideas to proofreading.

> Part 3, "The Research Paper," tells you how to conduct a research project with confidence. It also offers instruction for writing literature papers.

> Part 4, "Growing as a Writer," will help you to develop a clear, strong style of writing.

You won't necessarily use these parts in order because the process of writing does not follow a set sequence. Generating ideas, organizing, revising, and correcting all happen at several points along the way.

Rules of Thumb doesn't attempt to cover every little detail of grammar and usage, but it does cover the most common problems we've seen as teachers of writing over the past thirty years. We chose the phrase "rules of thumb" because it means a quick guide. The top part of your thumb is roughly an inch long. Sometimes you need a ruler, marked in millimeters, but sometimes you can do fine by measuring with just your thumb. Your thumb takes only a second to use, and it's always with you. We hope you'll find *Rules of Thumb* just as easy and comfortable to use.

Jay Silverman
Elaine Hughes
Diana Roberts Wienbroer

New to the Fifth Edition of *Rules of Thumb*

- An entirely new section (including six new chapters) on the research paper
- Coverage of APA and Chicago as well as MLA documentation styles
- A four-page "List of Valuable Sources" for research papers
- New chapters on "Addressing Your Audience" and "Using Strong Verbs"
- An expanded chapter on "Writing about Literature," now including research papers about literature
- Special features: "Sizing Up a Website" and "When You Find Too Many or Too Few Sources"
- For easy reference, 21 chapters and special features are either one page long or appear on two facing pages—see, for example, "Commas."

PART 1

CORRECTNESS

A Word about Correctness

Too much concern about correctness can inhibit your writing; too little concern can come between you and your readers. Don't let the fear of errors dominate the experience of writing for you. On the other hand, we would be misleading you if we told you that correctness doesn't matter. Basic errors in writing will distract and turn off even the most determined readers. We encourage you to master the rules presented here as quickly as possible so that you can feel secure about your writing. Once that happens, you'll be free to concentrate on what you want to say.

Confusing Words

A spellchecker won't catch these words. Find the ones that give you trouble and learn those.

a	Use before words starting with consonant sounds or long *u* (*a* bat, *a* coat, *a* union).
an	Use before words starting with vowels or pronounced as if they did (*an* age, *an* egg, *an* hour, *an* M&M).
accept	To take, to receive
	Most people do not accept criticism gracefully.
except	Not including
	Everybody except the piano player stopped playing.
affect	To change or influence
	Even nonprescription drugs can affect us in significant ways.
effect	The result, the consequence
	Effect is usually a noun, so you'll find *the* or *an* in front.
	Scientists have studied the effects of aspirin on heart disease.
conscience	The sense of right and wrong
	His conscience was clear.
conscious	Aware
	Flora became conscious of someone else in the room.
etc.	Abbreviation of *et cetera* (Latin for "and so forth"). The *c* is at the end, followed by a period. Don't write *and etc.*

We bought beads, confetti, serpentine, fireworks, etc., for Mardi Gras.

good, well   Test by trying your sentence with both. If *well* fits, use it.

Maybloom plays third base well.

Maybloom is a good third baseman.

But note these tricky cases:

Olivia looks good. (She's good looking.)

Rivka looks well. (She's no longer sick.)

Clara sees well. (Her eyes work.)

it's   It is. Test by substituting *it is.*

It's time to find a new solution.

its   Possessive

Every goat is attached to its own legs.

No apostrophe. *It is* cannot be substituted.

lay   To put something down

-ing: She is laying the cards on the table.

Past tense: He laid the cards on the table.

Once you *lay* something down, it *lies* there.

lie   To recline

As a child, I loved to lie in the hammock.

Past tense (here's the tricky part): lay One day I lay in the hammock for five hours.

Lied always means "told a lie."

lying   Reclining

Cleopatra was lying on a silken pillow.

Staying in place

The cards were lying on the table.

Telling a lie

The manufacturers were lying to the news media.

loose	Not tight
	After he lost thirty pounds, his jeans were all loose.
lose	To misplace
	I constantly lose my glasses.
	To be defeated
	I win; you lose.
no, new, now, know, knew	*No* is negative; new is not old; *now* is the present moment. *Know* and *knew* refer to knowledge.
of, have	Remember: *could have, should have, would have*—or *would've*—not *would of*
passed	A course, a car, a football; also *passed away (died)*
	Kirtley passed me on the street; he also passed English.
	Saturday he passed for two touchdowns.
	The coach passed away.
past	Yesterdays (the past; past events); also, *beyond*
	Rousseau could never forget his past romances.
	You can't rewrite the past.
	Go two miles past the railroad tracks.
quiet	Spike Jones rarely played quiet music.
quit	Mrs. Salvatore quit her job the day she won the lottery.
quite	Hippos move quite fast, considering their bulk.
than	Comparison
	I'd rather dance than eat.
then	Next
	She then added a drop of water.

their	Something is theirs.
	They never checked their facts.
	Wild dogs care for their young communally.
there	*A place:* Go over there.
	There is; there are; there was; there were
	There are several theories to explain Napoleon's retreat.
they're	They are.
	They're not in a position to negotiate
to	*Direction:* Give it to me. Go to New York.
	A verb form: To see, to run, to be (Note that you barely pronounce *to*.)
too	*More than enough:* Too hot, too bad, too late, too much.
	Also: Me, too! (Note that you pronounce *too* clearly.)
two	2
were	*Past tense:* You were, we were, they were.
we're	*We are:* We're a nation of immigrants.
where	*A place:* Where were you when the lights went out?
whether	*If*—not *weather* (rain or snow)
	No one knows whether or not he was murdered.
who's	*Who is:* Who's there? Who's coming with us?
whose	*Possessive:* Whose diamond is this?
woman	One person
	For the first time, a woman was named as CEO.
women	Several of them
	This woman is different from all other women.

Remember: *a* wom*a*n; *a* m*a*n

your	Belonging to you. Use only for your house, your car—*not* when you mean *you are.*
	Your relationship with your family changes when you marry.
you're	You are.
	You're going to question my logic.

ONE WORD OR TWO?

If you can put another word between them, you'll know to keep them separate. Otherwise, you'll have to check them one by one.

a lot	Always written as two words
	A lot of teachers—a whole lot—find "a lot" too informal.
all ready	We were all ready for Grandpa's wedding.
already	Those crooks have already taken their percentage.
all right	Always two words
a long	Childhood seems like a long time.
along	They walked along the Navajo Trail.
a part	I want a part of the American pie.
apart	The twins were rarely apart.
at least	Always two words
each other	Always two words
even though	Always two words
everybody	Jimmy's comments incensed everybody in the chat room. (*Every body* means *every corpse.*)
every day	It rains every day, every single day.
everyday	Fernando put on his everyday clothes.
every one	Every one of the beavers survived the flood.
everyone	Everyone likes pizza.
in depth	Always two words
in fact	Always two words
in order	Always two words
in spite of	Always three words
intact	Always one word
into	Always one word

in touch	Always two words
itself	Always one word
myself	Always one word
nobody	Nobody knows how Mr. Avengail makes his money. (*No body* refers to a corpse.)
no one	Always two words
nowadays	Always one word
nevertheless	Always one word
somehow	Always one word
some time sometimes	I need some time alone. Sometimes your mouth can get you into trouble.
throughout	Always one word
whenever	Always one word
whereas	Always one word
wherever	Always one word
withheld	Always one word
without	Always one word

Hyphenated Words

- Hyphens are used in compound words.

    self-employed
    in-laws
    seventy-five
    happy-go-lucky

- Hyphens make a multiple-word adjective before a noun, but not after it.

    Alfred Hitchcock is a well-known filmmaker.
    Alfred Hitchcock is well known as a filmmaker.

    George Eliot was a nineteenth-century author.
    George Eliot wrote in the nineteenth century.

    The trip was a once-in-a-lifetime opportunity.
    An opportunity like this comes only once in a lifetime.

SPELLING

There's no getting around it. Correct spelling takes patience. But you can save time by learning the rules that fit your errors and by using a spellcheck on a computer.

I Before *E*

Use *I* before *E*
Except after *C*
Or when sounded like A
As in *neighbor* and *weigh*.

bel*ie*ve	dece*i*ve	fre*i*ght
fr*ie*nd	rece*i*ve	ve*i*n
p*ie*ce	conce*i*t	

Exceptions:

we*i*rd   fore*i*gn   le*i*sure   se*i*ze   the*i*r

Word Endings

The quiet *-ed* endings:

Three *-ed* endings are not always pronounced clearly, but they need to be written.

used to   supposed to   prejudiced

-sk and *-st* endings:

When *s* is added to words like these, it isn't always clearly pronounced, but it still needs to be there.

asks	consists	psychologists
risks	insists	scientists
desks	suggests	terrorists
tasks	costs	interests

The -*y* endings:

When a verb ends in *y*, keep the *y* when you add *ing*. To add *s* or *ed*, change the *y* to *i*.

crying	cries	cried
studying	studies	studied
trying	tries	tried

When a noun ends in *y*, make it plural by changing the *y* to *i* and adding *es*.

activities	families	theories

Exception: Simply add *s* to nouns ending in *ey*.

attorneys	monkeys	valleys

p or pp? t or tt?

Listen to the *vowel before* the added part.

If the vowel sounds like its own letter name, *use only one consonant:*

writer	writing

The *i* sounds like the name of the letter *i*, so you use one *t*.

If the vowel before the added part has a different sound from its name, *double the consonant:*

written

The *i* sounds like the *i* in *it*, so you double the *t*.

The same method works for *hoping* and *hopping*. Listen for the different sounds of the letter *o*.

Here are some other examples:

beginning	dropping	quitting
stopped	occurred	referred

An exception: *coming*.

Words with Prefixes and Suffixes

When you add a prefix or suffix, you usually keep the spelling of the root word.

*mi*sspell	sudden*ness*	*dis*satisfaction
hope*ful*	*dis*appear	govern*ment*
*un*noticed	environ*ment*	

The *-ly* endings also follow this rule.

really	totally	lonely
finally	unfortunately	usually

But *truly* does not follow the rule.
Exception: The final *e* is usually dropped before a suffix that starts with a vowel.

debata*ble*	sens*ible*	lov*able*

Tricky Words

Look hard at the middle of each word:

de*fini*tely	em*barr*ass	in*ter*est
se*pa*rate	ac*com*modate	ne*cess*ary
re*pet*ition	pro*bab*ly	fam*ili*ar
o*pin*ion		

Capitalization

Capitalize the first letter of every sentence and of names of people, localities, days of the week, and months. Do not capitalize for emphasis.

Do Capitalize

- Subjects in school whose names come from names of countries; complete titles of courses

    English　　　Spanish　　　History 101

- In titles, the first word, major words, and words of six letters or more

    The Red and the Black　　　*Men Against the Sea*

- Family names like *Mother, Aunt,* or *Grandfather* only when used as a name or with a name (but not after *my, his, her, their, our*)

    Papa was cared for by Uncle Manny after my mother left.

- Days of the week

    Wednesday　　　Saturday

- People's titles when they precede their names

    Dr. Judd　　　Officer Zublonski　　　Major Gross

- Brand names

    Kleenex　　　Coca-Cola　　　Domino's Pizza

- Public holidays

    Thanksgiving　　　Fourth of July

- The entire name of a specific place, event, and so forth

    Oak Street　　　Battle of Gettysburg　　　Calhoun High School

Do Not Capitalize

- Subjects in school whose names do not come from the names of countries

    history   psychology   marketing

- Genres of literature and art

    novel   poetry   gangster movies   jazz

- Family names like *mother, aunt, grandfather* after *a, the, my, his, her, their, our*

    my mother   his aunt   the grandmother

- Seasons of the year

    spring   autumn

- Titles of people separate from their names

    I went to the doctor.
    Two generals and an admiral were consulted.

- Generic names

    facial tissues   soda pop   pizza

- Private celebrations

    birthday   anniversary

- A type of place, event, and so forth

    a dark street   the eve of battle   high school

- For emphasis

    Do not capitalize whole words (AMNESIA); do not capitalize an entire essay or Internet message.

ABBREVIATIONS AND NUMBERS

Avoid abbreviations, except for words that are always abbreviated.
Spell out numbers that take only a word or two.

▪ ABBREVIATIONS

- As a general rule, don't abbreviate—especially don't use abbreviations like these in your papers:

dept.	yr.	NY	Eng.	Thurs.	b / c
w / o	co.	&	gov't.	Prof.	thru

- But do abbreviate words that you *always* see abbreviated, such as certain titles with proper names and well-known organizations:

Mr. Smith	FBI
St. Bartholomew	IBM

- Abbreviate *doctor* only before a name:

the doctor	Dr. Salk

▪ NUMBERS

Spell Out

- Numbers that take only one or two words

nine	twenty-seven	two billion

- Numbers that begin a sentence

  One hundred four years ago the ship sank.
  The ship sank 104 years ago.

- Numbers that form a compound word

  a two-year-old baby

- Fractions

  one-half

Use Numerals for

- Numbers that require three or more words

    1,889   162

- Dates, page references, room numbers, statistics, addresses, percentages, and dollars and cents

    May 6, 1974   7,500 residents   99.44%
    page 2   221B Baker Street $5.98

- A list or series of numbers

    1, 4, 9, 16, 25
    seats 12, 14, and 16

- Papers on scientific or technical subjects

APOSTROPHES

Most of the time, when you add an *s* to a word you don't need an apostrophe. Use apostrophes for contractions and possessives.

Do Not Add an Apostrophe; Just Add *s* or *es*

To make a plural

Two bosses   Three dogs   Five families

To a present-tense verb

He sees.   She says.   It talks.   Carol sings.

Look hard at *sees* and *says:* no apostrophe.

Add an Apostrophe

To a contraction (put the apostrophe where the missing letter was)

doesn't = does not	it's = it is	that's
don't	I'm	weren't
didn't	you're	what's

To a possessive

my mother's car	Baldwin's style	a night's sleep
Gus's hair	children's toys	a family's history
Ms. Jones's opinion	women's room	today's world

- If the word is plural and already ends with *s,* just add an apostrophe after the *s.*

    my friends' apartment (several friends)
    my grandparents' dishes

- Pronouns in possessive form have *no* apostrophe.

    its   hers   his   ours   theirs   yours

CONSISTENT PRONOUNS

Make a conscious choice of your pronouns. Don't shift from *a person* to *they* to *you* to *I*.

The problem comes with sentences like

> I got mad; it does make you feel upset when people don't listen.

> A young person has to manage their time well if they want to get ahead.

> I know someone rich, and they are not happy.

A person and *someone* are singular; *they* and *their* are plural. Mixing these words in one sentence leads to awkward writing and creates errors. Nowadays you will hear this usage in conversation and will even see it in print, but it is still not acceptable in most writing.

Study the following options:

people . . . they	Instead of *a person* or *someone,* try *people* (which fits with *they*).
	> When people know what they want, they can be firm.
a real person	Better yet, use a true-to-life example, a real person.
	> My cousin Marc is rich, but he is not happy.
	A real example not only makes the grammar correct, but it is also much more interesting and memorable. *A person* and *someone* are nobodies.
he, he or she	The old-fashioned pronoun choice to accompany *a person* is *he.*
	> If a person is strong, he stands up for his beliefs, even against a majority.

But this choice presumes that *a person* is male. It should be avoided because it is sexist language. *He or she* is possible, but not if it comes several times in a row; *he or she,* when repeated, becomes clunky and awkward.

> If a person is strong, he or she stands up for his or her beliefs, even against a majority.

Avoid *he/she* and *s/he.*

I   Don't be afraid of *I.* It is very strong in writing about emotions and experience. In these matters, being objective is not as good as being truthful. As Thoreau wrote, "I should not talk so much about myself if there were anybody else whom I knew as well." A lot of times when you generalize, you really are writing from experience. If you speak for yourself, often you will get to the nitty-gritty of the subject—what you know to be true.

> If I were strong, I would stand up for my beliefs, even against a majority.

You don't, however, need phrases like *I think* or *in my opinion* because the whole paper is, after all, what you choose to say.

you   *You* is good for giving directions and writing letters. It establishes an intimate tone with your reader. For essays, however, it may seem too informal or too preachy.

> If you are strong, you stand up for your beliefs, even against a majority.

Try *we* instead, when you mean *people in general.*

> If we are strong, we stand up for our beliefs, even against a majority.

In any case, beware of mixing pronouns.

> Riding my bicycle is good for your legs.

one   *One* means a person—singular. If you use it, you must stick with it.

> If one is strong, one stands up for one's beliefs, even against a majority.

One is an option for solving the *he/she* problem; it is appropriate for formal writing. Nevertheless, when repeated, *one* can sound stuffy. How many times can one say *one* before one makes oneself sound silly?

we   *We* can be used to mean *people in general.*

> If we are strong, we stand up for our beliefs, even against a majority.

Be careful that you mean more than just yourself. Using *I* might be more appropriate.

they   *They* is often the best solution to the *he/she* problem, but remember that *they* must refer to a plural, such as *many people* or *some people.*

> If people are strong, they stand up for their beliefs, even against a majority.

no pronoun   Often you can avoid the problem entirely. Instead of

> A young person has to manage his or her time well if he or she wants to get ahead.

write:

> A young person has to manage time well to get ahead.

CORRECT PRONOUNS

I, she, he, we, they, and *who* identify the persons doing the action. *Me, her, him, us, them,* and *whom* identify the persons receiving the action.

Pairs: My Friends and I / My Friends and Me

- With a pair of people, try the sentence without the other person:

  > My friends and I saw the movie six times.
  > (. . . I saw the movie, *not* Me saw the movie.)

  > Carter gave the tickets to my friends and me.
  > (Carter gave the tickets to me, *not* to I.)

  The same rule goes for *him, her, he, she.*

  > The friar mixed a potion for Romeo and her.
  > (He mixed the potion for her, *not* for she.)

  Note: Put yourself last in a list:

  > My brothers and I fought constantly.
  > (*Not* Me and my brothers fought constantly.)

  > Beverly read her story to Noah, Hannah, and me.

  Don't be afraid of *me;* it's often right.

  > Between you and me, Mickey is heading for a fall.
  > (*Not* Between you and I . . .)

- Don't use *myself* when *me* will do.

  > I painted the whole apartment myself.
  > (Here, *me* cannot be substituted.)

  > Sam did the formatting for Toby and me.
  > (*Not* . . . for Toby and myself.)

  Never write *themself;* use *themselves.*

Comparisons

- Use *I, he, she, we, they* when comparing with the subject of the sentence—usually the first person in the sentence.

  Phil was more generous to Sarah than I was.
  Zachary is more nervous than she is.

  Sometimes *is* is left off the end:

  Zachary is more nervous than she.

- Use *me, him, her, us, them* when comparing with the receiver, the object of the sentence—usually the person mentioned later in the sentence.

  Phil was more generous to Sarah than to me.

  Note the difference:

  He was nastier to Ramona than I.

  (He was nastier to Ramona than I was.)

  He was nastier to Ramona than me.

  (He was nastier to Ramona than to me.)

Who / Whom

- Use *whom* after prepositions (to whom, of whom, for whom, from whom, with whom).

  To whom should I address my complaint?

- Use *who* for subjects of verbs.

  Who should I say is calling?

  When in doubt, use *who.*

Vague Pronouns

Certain pronouns—*which, it, this, that,* and *who*—must refer to a single word, not to a whole phrase. Keep them near the word they refer to.

These words are used loosely in conversation, but in most writing you should use them more precisely.

Which

Which causes the most trouble of the five. Don't overuse it.

> *Imprecise:* Last week I felt sick in which I didn't even get to go to school.
>
> *Precise:* Last week I felt sick. I didn't even get to go to school.
>
> *Precise:* Last week I had a cold which kept me from going to school.

In the last example, *which* clearly refers to *cold.*

Use *in which* only when you mean that one thing is inside the other:

> The box in which I keep my jewelry fell apart.

Note that *which* normally cannot start a sentence unless it asks a question.

It

When you use *it,* make sure the reader knows what *it* is. *It* is often weak at the start of a sentence when *it* refers to nothing.

> *Imprecise:* Eleanore ate a big Chinese dinner and then had a chocolate milk shake for dessert. *It* made her sick.
>
> *Precise:* Eleanore ate a big Chinese dinner and then had a chocolate milk shake for dessert. The *combination* made her sick.

This

This cannot refer to a whole situation or a group of things, so insert a word after *this* to sum up what *this* refers to.

> *Imprecise:* She never calls me, she's never ready when I pick her up for a date, and she forgot my birthday. *This* makes me angry.

> *Precise:* She never calls me, she's never ready when I pick her up for a date, and she forgot my birthday. This *behavior* makes me angry.

That

Just like *this, that* cannot refer to a whole situation or a group of things. When *that* seems unclear, replace it with what it stands for.

> *Imprecise:* We are not paid well and receive inadequate benefits, but I don't think we should discuss *that* yet.

The reader might ask, "Discuss *what* yet?"

> *Precise:* We are not paid well and receive inadequate benefits, but I don't think we should discuss *benefits* yet.

Who

Use *who* for people—not *which.*

> The runner who finished last got all the publicity.

RECOGNIZING COMPLETE SENTENCES

At the heart of every sentence—no matter how complicated—is a subject-verb combination.

To recognize a complete sentence, you need to recognize its true subject and verb.

■ SIMPLE SENTENCES

- A sentence always has a *subject* and a *verb:*

  > I won.
  > Phillippe snores.
  > This soup is cold.

  I, Phillippe, soup are the subjects; *won, snores, is* are the verbs. Notice that the verb enables the subject to *do* or *be* something.

  These very short sentences have only a one-word subject and a one-word verb.

- Usually a word or phrase completes the subject and verb:

  > Janeen walks three miles a day.
  >
  > Suzanne spent all of her savings.
  >
  > It's not very difficult.
  >
  > She says absolutely nothing.
  >
  > They had headaches for two days.
  >
  > Robert is my latest fiancé.
  >
  > The "blow torch murders" were committed by the least likely suspect—the grandmother.
  >
  > High above the Kona coast in Hawaii stands one of the world's great chocolate plantations.

- Sentences can have more than one subject and more than one verb:

  Tracy and Pete have a new home. (two subjects)

  They bought an old house and restored it. (two verbs)

- Sometimes the subject is understood to be "you," the reader; the sentence is usually a command or a direction:

  Avoid submerging this product in water.

  Walk two blocks past the traffic light.

- Sometimes a word or group of words introduces the main part of a sentence:

  However, the bar is closed.

  For example, chemists write CO_2 instead of *carbon dioxide*.

  Then we drove a thousand miles.

  At the end of the game, the umpire and the pitcher got into a fight.

  In the cabin by the lake, you'll find the paddles and life jackets.

For more information about recognizing subjects and verbs, see "Verb Agreement," page 47.

■ COMPOUND OR COORDINATE SENTENCES

Two complete sentences can be joined to make a *compound,* or *coordinate,* sentence.

- Sometimes the two sentences are joined by a comma and one of the following connecting words:

and	so	or	for
but	yet	nor	

  Janeen walks three miles a day, but she still eats junk food.

  Suzanne spent all of her savings, and now she has to start using her credit cards.

- Sometimes the two sentences are connected by a semicolon.

  Grasshoppers are lazy; they are not very hard to catch.

■ COMPLEX OR SUBORDINATE SENTENCES

Sometimes a sentence has two parts—the main part (a complete short sentence) and a *subordinated* part (a complete short sentence preceded by a *subordinating* word, such as *because, although, if, when, after,* or *while*).

> Suzanne has spent all of her savings because her brother is ill.
>
> Mona shouts when she talks on the telephone.
>
> The primary market for sea urchins is Japan although they are harvested in Maine.

Notice in the first sentence that "Suzanne has spent all of her savings" could be a complete sentence. On the other hand, "because her brother is ill" is not complete by itself. In the second sentence, "when she talks on the telephone" is also incomplete. In the third sentence, "although they are harvested in Maine" is incomplete.

The two parts of each sentence are reversible:

> Because her brother is ill, Suzanne has spent all of her savings.
>
> When she talks on the telephone, Mona shouts.
>
> Although sea urchins are harvested in Maine, the primary market is Japan.

A *compound-complex sentence* occurs when one or both halves of a compound sentence have subordinated parts.

> Suzanne always seemed to be a skinflint, but she has spent all her savings because her brother is ill.

Run-on Sentences and Sentence Fragments

To decide whether to use a period or a comma, look at what comes before and after the punctuation.

Often you reach a pause in your writing, and you wonder, "Do I put a comma or a period?" The length of a sentence has nothing to do with the right choice. You need to look at what comes before and after the punctuation to see whether you have two separate sentences or a single sentence with a fragment attached to it.

■ Recognizing Run-on Sentences (Comma Splices and Fused Sentences)

The most common run-on sentence happens when you have two complete sentences, but you have only a comma or no punctuation between them. Run-ons usually occur because the two sentences are closely related. Run-on sentences are sometimes called *comma splices* (two sentences with only a comma between them) or *fused sentences* (two sentences with no punctuation between them).

The two most common spots where run-ons occur are

* When a pronoun begins the second sentence:

    Incorrect: The light floated toward us, it gave an eerie glow.

    Correct:　The light floated toward us. It gave an eerie glow.

    Incorrect: Ralph decided to move to Paris, he wanted to be a writer.

    Correct:　Ralph decided to move to Paris. He wanted to be a writer.

- When *however* begins the second sentence:

   Incorrect: Mosquitoes in the United States are just an annoyance, however in many countries they are a health hazard.

   Correct: Mosquitoes in the United States are just an annoyance. However, in many countries they are a health hazard.

How to Fix Run-on Sentences

   Incorrect: I went to Gorman's Ice Cream Parlor, I ordered a triple hot fudge sundae.

   Suzanne spent all of her savings now she is flat broke.

- The simplest way to fix a run-on sentence is to put a period or semicolon between the two sentences:

   Correct: I went to Gorman's Ice Cream Parlor. I ordered a triple hot fudge sundae.

   Suzanne spent all of her savings. Now she is flat broke.

(Remember that it is perfectly correct to have two or three short sentences in a row.)

   Correct: I went to Gorman's Ice Cream Parlor; I ordered a triple hot fudge sundae.

   Suzanne spent all of her savings; now she is flat broke.

- Here are two other ways to fix run-on sentences:

Put a comma and a conjunction between the two sentences. The conjunctions are *and, but, so, yet, for, or,* and *nor.*

   Correct: I went to Gorman's Ice Cream Parlor, and I ordered a triple hot fudge sundae.

   Suzanne spent all of her savings, so now she is flat broke.

Use a subordinating word with one of the sentences:

Correct: I went to Gorman's Ice Cream Parlor, where I ordered a triple hot fudge sundae.

Because Suzanne spent all of her savings, now she is flat broke.

Other run-on sentences just go on and on, strung together with *and* and *but*. These need to be divided into two or more shorter sentences.

■ RECOGNIZING SENTENCE FRAGMENTS

Many sentence fragments may appear to be complete sentences, but they have elements that make them incomplete.

Words That Rarely Begin Sentences

Certain words *almost never* begin sentences:

such as	which	
especially	who	
not	whose	except in a question
like, just like	how	
the same as	what	

In addition, if you have trouble with sentence fragments, it's best not to start sentences with *and* or *but*.

In most cases, put a comma or a dash before these words.

Incorrect: We had to drain the pipes after every vacation. Especially in the winter.

Correct: We had to drain the pipes after every vacation— especially in the winter.

Incorrect: They gave me one lousy dollar. Which was a full day's pay.

Correct: They gave me one lousy dollar, which was a full day's pay.

Incorrect: N. C. Wyeth illustrated many children's books. Such as Jules Verne's *The Mysterious Island*.

Correct: N. C. Wyeth illustrated many children's books, such as Jules Verne's *The Mysterious Island*.

Subordinating Words

Certain words always begin *half* a sentence—either the first half or the second half. These are called *subordinating words:*

when	if
before	because
after	although (even though)
as	unless
while	whereas

A sentence fragment frequently begins with a subordinating word.

> *Incorrect:* Although Janeen walks three miles a day.
>
> When Archduke Franz Ferdinand was assassinated in Sarajevo.

You can fix these fragments by connecting each fragment to the sentence before or after it.

> *Correct:* Although Janeen walks three miles a day, she still has to watch her diet.
>
> Janeen still has to watch her diet although she walks three miles a day.
>
> When Archduke Franz Ferdinand was assassinated in Sarajevo, the whole world was plunged into war.
>
> The whole world was plunged into war when Archduke Franz Ferdinand was assassinated in Sarajevo.

You can also drop the subordinating word.

> *Correct:* Janeen walks three miles a day.
>
> Archduke Franz Ferdinand was assassinated in Sarajevo.

A subtle point: Watch out for *and*. Putting *and* between a fragment and a sentence doesn't fix the fragment.

> *Still*
>
> *Incorrect:* Although Janeen walks three miles a day and she still watches her diet.
>
> *Correct:* Although Janeen walks three miles a day and she still watches her diet, she has not yet reached her goal.

Verbs Ending in *-ing*

Verbs ending in *-ing* cannot serve as the main verb of a sentence:

> *Incorrect:* The boys ran toward the ocean. Leaping across the hot sand.
>
> I have three good friends. One being my cousin.
>
> I love walking in the evening and taking in nature's beauty. The sun setting over the prairie. The wind blowing the tall grass.

One solution is to connect the fragment to the preceding sentence.

> *Correct:* The boys ran toward the ocean, leaping across the hot sand.
>
> I love walking in the evening and taking in nature's beauty—the sun setting over the prairie and the wind blowing the tall grass.

The second solution is to change the *-ing* verb to a complete verb.

> *Correct:* They leaped across the hot sand.
>
> One is my cousin.

An *-ing* verb *can* begin a sentence if a complete verb comes later.

> *Correct:* Leaping across the hot sand hurts my feet.

To Verbs

To verbs *(to be, to feel)* also frequently begin fragments.

> *Incorrect:* I went back home to talk to my father. To tell him how I felt.
>
> Keep this hairdryer away from the sink. To avoid submersion in water.

Fix these fragments by connecting them to the sentence before or by adding a subject and verb:

> *Correct:* I went back home to talk to my father, to tell him how I felt.
>
> I went back home to talk to my father. I needed to tell him how I felt.
>
> Keep this hairdryer away from the sink to avoid submersion in water.

> Keep this hairdryer away from the sink. You must avoid submerging it in water.

A *to* verb can begin a sentence if a complete verb comes later.

> *Correct:* To talk to my father always calms me down.

Repeated Words

A repeated word can create a fragment.

> *Incorrect:* Elizabeth's the ideal cat. A cat who both plays and purrs.
>
> I believe that Whitman is our greatest poet. That he singlehandedly began modern American poetry.

The best solution here is to replace the period with a comma.

> *Correct:* Elizabeth's the ideal cat, a cat who both plays and purrs.
>
> I believe that Whitman is our greatest poet, that he singlehandedly began modern American poetry.

Note: *That* rarely begins a sentence, except when it points, as in "That was the year of the great flood."

Using Fragments for Style

You will notice that professional writers sometimes use sentence fragments for emphasis or style. Be sure you have control over fragments before you experiment. In the right spot, a fragment can be very strong.

Using *But, However, Although*

> These three words are used to reverse the meaning of a sentence, **but** they are punctuated differently.
>
> These three words are used to reverse the meaning of a sentence; **however,** they are punctuated differently.
>
> These three words are used to reverse the meaning of a sentence **although** they are punctuated differently.

For further options in using *however,* see pages 35 and 36. For further options in using *although,* see page 27.

COMMAS

More errors come from having too many commas than from having too few. Here are four places you need them.

Comma before *but, and, so, yet, or, for,* and *nor*

Put a comma before *but, and, so, yet, or, for,* and *nor* when they connect two sentences.

> The lead actor was on crutches, but the show went on.
>
> Gina intended to win the weight-lifting pageant, and that's exactly what she did.
>
> Not only did Melva run a restaurant, but she also wrote a cookbook.
>
> The house didn't sell at $300,000, so they lowered the price.

However, don't automatically stick in a comma just because a sentence is long.

> No one at the paint factory could have guessed that the boss would one day be a famous writer.

Commas in a List or Series

Use commas between parts of a series of three or more.

> In one month the game farm saved the lives of a red fox, a great-horned owl, and a black bear cub.
>
> Diamond climbed up the ladder, marched to the end of the diving board, took a big spring, and came down in a belly bust.
>
> In the class sat a bearded man, a police officer, a woman eating a sandwich, and a parakeet.

(Without the last comma, what happens to the parakeet?)

Don't use a comma in a pair.

> In one month the game farm saved the lives of a red fox and a great-horned owl.
>
> Mary Ellen's mother handed out hard candies and made us sit while she played Mozart's "Turkish March" on the piano.

Comma after a Lead-in

Use a comma after an introductory part of a sentence.

Sometimes the lead-in is just a word or a phrase.

> However, the truth finally came out.
>
> For example, you can learn how to fix a leaky faucet.
>
> After lunch, she gave me a cup of that terrible herb tea.

Sometimes the lead-in is an entire clause that begins with a subordinating word (such as *when, after, if, because,* or *although*). In this case, the comma comes at the turning point of the sentence.

> When James walked through the front door, the whole family was laughing hysterically.
>
> If one of the brain's two hemispheres is damaged early in life, the healthy one often takes on the functions of both.

A Pair of Commas around an Insertion

Surround an insertion or interruption with a *pair* of commas. Both commas are necessary.

> The truth, however, finally came out.
>
> Woody Guthrie, the father of Arlo Guthrie, wrote "This Land Is Your Land."
>
> My cousin, who thinks she is always right, was dead wrong.
>
> Milton, even though no one had invited him, arrived first at the party.
>
> In "The Raven," by Edgar Allan Poe, the bird gradually takes on more and more meaning for the narrator.

Note in the last example that the comma goes inside the quotation marks.

Places and *dates* are treated as insertions. Note especially that commas surround the year and the state.

> The hospital was in Oshkosh, Wisconsin, not far from Omro.
> I was born on August 15, 1954, at seven in the morning.

SEMICOLONS

Semicolons can be used instead of periods; they also can separate parts of a complicated list.

- Use a semicolon to connect two related sentences; each half must be a complete sentence.

    Ask for what you want; accept what you get.

    One day she says she's at death's door; the next day she's ready to rock and roll.

    I'll never forget the night of the circus; that's when I met the trapeze artist who changed my life.

    It's not that O'Hara's position is wrong; it's that he misses the key point.

    A semicolon often comes before certain transition words; a comma follows the transition.

however	therefore	otherwise
nevertheless	in other words	instead
for example	on the other hand	meanwhile
besides	furthermore	unfortunately

    Schubert was a great composer; however, Beethoven was greater.

    The bank lost two of my deposits; therefore, I am closing my account.

    Semicolons work best when used to emphasize a strong connection between the two sentences.

- Use semicolons instead of commas in a list when some of the parts already have commas.

    As a child, what your friends have, you want to have; what they do, you want to do; and where they go, you want to go.

Colons create suspense: they signal that an example, a quotation, or an explanation will follow.

Use a colon after a complete sentence to introduce related details.

Before a colon you must have a *complete statement*. Don't use a colon after *are* or *include* or *such as*.

Colons can introduce

- A list

    First, you need the basic supplies: a tent, a sleeping bag, a cooking kit, and a backpack.

- A quotation

    The author begins with a shocker: "Mother spent her summer sitting naked on a rock."

- An example

    Vegetarians often use legumes: for example, beans or lentils.

- An emphatic assertion

    This is the bottom line: I refuse to work for less than $10.00 an hour.

- A subtitle

    Rules of Thumb: A Guide for Writers

When you type, leave two spaces after a colon.

Dashes and Parentheses

Dashes and parentheses separate a word or remark from the rest of the sentence.

■ Dashes

Dashes highlight the part of the sentence they separate, or show an abrupt change of thought in mid-sentence, or connect a fragment to a sentence.

> Alberta Hunter--still singing at the age of eighty--performed nightly at The Cookery in New York City.

> At night the forest is magical and fascinating--and yet it terrifies me.

> Living the high life--that's what I want.

Dashes are very handy; they can replace a period, comma, colon, or semicolon. However, they are usually informal, so don't use many—or you will seem to have dashed off your paper.

When you type, two hyphens make a dash; there is no space before or after the dash. (Computers now can be set to provide a true "em dash.")

■ Parentheses

Parentheses deemphasize the words they separate. Use them to enclose brief explanations or interruptions. They can contain either part of a sentence or a whole sentence.

> I demanded reasonable working hours (nine to five), and they met my request.

> Bergman's last film disappointed the critics. (See the attached reviews.)

> Mayme drives slowly (she claims her car won't go over forty miles per hour), so she gets tickets for causing traffic jams.

- Put any necessary punctuation *after* the second parenthesis if the parentheses contain part of a sentence.

- If the parentheses contain a complete sentence, put the period *inside* the second parenthesis. Notice, however, that you don't capitalize or use a period when parentheses enclose a sentence within a sentence.

Be sparing with parentheses. Too many can chop up your sentences.

Quotation Marks

Use quotation marks any time you use someone else's exact words. If they are not the exact words, don't surround them with quotation marks.

Quotations in this chapter come from the following selection from Mark Twain's *Adventures of Huckleberry Finn:*

> Sometimes we'd have the whole river all to ourselves for the longest time. Yonder was the banks and the islands, across the water; and maybe a spark—which was a candle in a cabin window—and sometimes on the water you could see a spark or two—on a raft or a scow, you know; and maybe you could hear a fiddle or a song coming over from one of them crafts. It's lovely to live on a raft.

Punctuation before a Quotation

Here are three ways to lead into a quotation:

- For short quotations (a word or a phrase), don't use *Twain says,* and don't put a comma before the quotation. Simply use the writer's phrase as it fits smoothly into your sentence:

    Huck Finn finds it "lovely" to float down the Mississippi River on a raft.

- Put a comma before the quotation marks if you use *he says.*

    Huck says, "It's lovely to live on a raft."

    Put no comma before the quotation marks if you use *he says that.*

    Huck says that "It's lovely to live on a raft."

- Use a colon (:) before a quotation of a sentence or more. Be sure you have a complete statement before the colon. Don't use *he says.*

    In one short sentence, Twain pulls together the whole paragraph: "It's lovely to live on a raft."

Punctuation after a Quotation

At the end of a quotation, the period or comma goes *inside* the quotation marks. Do not close the quotation marks until the person's words end. Use one mark of punctuation to end your sentence—never two periods or a comma and a period.

> Twain writes, "you could hear a fiddle or a song coming over from one of them crafts. It's lovely to live on a raft."

Semicolons go outside of closing quotation marks.

> Huck says, "It's lovely to live on a raft"; however, this raft eventually drifts him into trouble.

Question marks and exclamation marks go inside if the person you are writing about is asking or exclaiming. (If *you* are asking or exclaiming, the mark goes outside.)

> "Have you read *Huckleberry Finn*?" she asked.
>
> Did Twain call Huck's life "lovely"?

When your quotation is more than a few words, let the quotation end your sentence. Otherwise you're liable to get a tangled sentence.

> *Tangled:* Huck says, "It's lovely to live on a raft" illustrates his love of freedom.
>
> *Correct:* Huck says, "It's lovely to live on a raft." This quotation illustrates his love of freedom.

(See pages 112–113 and 116–117 for a discussion of punctuation after quotations in research papers.)

Indenting Long Quotations

Long quotations (three or more lines) do not get quotation marks. Instead, start on a new line and indent the whole left margin of the quotation ten spaces. After the quotation, return to the original margin and continue your paragraph.

> Huck and Jim lead a life of ease:
>
> > Sometimes we'd have the whole river all to ourselves for the longest time. Yonder was the banks and the islands, across the water; and maybe a spark—which was a candle in a cabin window—and sometimes on the water you could

> see a spark or two—on a raft or a scow, you know;
> and maybe you could hear a fiddle or a song
> coming over from one of them crafts. It's lovely to
> live on a raft.

Brackets indicate that you have added or changed a word to make the quotation clear.

An **ellipsis** (three periods separated by spaces) within brackets indicates that you have left out words from the original quotation. Use a fourth period after the brackets to end your sentence.

> Sometimes we'd have that whole river [the
> Mississippi] all to ourselves for the longest time
> [. . .]. It's lovely to live on a raft.

You don't need an ellipsis at the beginning or end of a quotation, only when omitting words from the middle.

Dialogue

In dialogue, start a new paragraph every time you switch from one speaker to the other.

> "Did you enjoy reading *Huckleberry Finn?*" asked
> Professor Migliaccio.
> "I guess so," Joylene said, "but the grammar is awful."
> The professor thought a moment. "You know, the book
> was once banned in Boston because of that. I guess
> Twain's experiment still has some shock value."
> "Well, it shocked me," said Joylene. "I can't believe an
> educated man would write that way."

Writing about a Word or Phrase

When you discuss a word or phrase, surround it with quotation marks.

> The name "Mark Twain" means "two fathoms deep."

> Advertisers use "America," while news reporters refer to
> "the United States."

Do not use quotation marks around slang; either use the word without quotation marks or find a better word.

Quotation within a Quotation

For quotations within a quotation, use single quotation marks:

> According to radio announcer Rhingo Lake, "The jockey clearly screamed 'I've been foiled!' as the horse fell to the ground right before the finish line."

Quoting Poetry

For poetry, when quoting two or more lines, indent ten spaces from the left margin and copy the lines of poetry exactly as the poet arranged them.

> We are such stuff
> As dreams are made on; and our little life
> Is rounded with a sleep.

When a line of poetry is too long to fit on a line of your paper, indent the turnover line an additional three spaces, as in the following line from Walt Whitman's *Leaves of Grass.*

> I believe that a leaf of grass is no less than the
> journeywork of the stars.

When quoting a *few* words of poetry that include a line break, use a slash mark to show where the poet's line ends.

> In *The Tempest*, Shakespeare calls us "such stuff / As dreams are made on."

Titles: Underlines, Italics, or Quotation Marks

Underline or italicize titles of longer works and use quotation marks for titles of shorter works.

- <u>Underline</u> or *italicize* titles of longer works, such as books, magazines, plays, newspapers, movies, and television programs.

  <u>War and Peace</u>   <u>CBS Reports</u>

  <u>The New York Times</u> <u>The Wizard of Oz</u>

  Underlining and italics are equivalent, but don't mix them in your paper. For MLA or APA research styles, you should underline; for Chicago style or posting a paper online, you should italicize.

- Put "quotation marks" around titles of shorter works, such as short stories, articles, poems, songs, and chapter titles.

  "The Star-Spangled Banner"

  "The Pit and the Pendulum"

  Remember that a comma or period, if needed, goes inside the quotation marks.

  In "Stopping by Woods on a Snowy Evening," Robert Frost uses an intricate rhyme scheme.

- Do not underline or place quotation marks around your title on a cover sheet—unless your title contains someone else's title.

  My Week on a Shrimp Boat

  An Analysis of T. S. Eliot's "The Love Song of J. Alfred Prufrock"

  The Vision of War in <u>The Red Badge of Courage</u>

- Capitalize only the first word and all major words in a title.

SHIFTING VERB TENSES

Sometimes you may find yourself slipping back and forth between present and past verb tenses. Be consistent, especially within each paragraph.

Present Tense for Literature

Use the present tense for writing about literature, film, and the arts.

> Scarlett comes into the room and pulls down the draperies.
>
> Hamlet speaks with irony even about death.

Past Tense for True Stories

Use the simple past tense to tell your own stories or stories from history.

> On a dare, I jumped off the back of the garage.
>
> President Truman waved from the caboose.

Troublesome Verbs

Had

Many people use *had* when they don't need it. Use *had* to refer to events that were already finished when your story or example took place—the past before the past that you're describing. To check, try adding *previously* or *already* next to *had*.

> In 1986, we moved to New York. We had lived in Florida for three years.
>
> If I had known about tse-tse flies, I would have been much more cautious.

Would

- Use *would* for something that happened regularly during a period of the past.

> In the early days of automobiles, tires frequently would blow out.

- Use *would* when writing in the past tense and referring to something that at that time was projected for the future.

  > The producer promised his niece that she would get the lead in the movie. (*Not* she will get the lead)

- Use *would* for hypothetical situations.

  > Elaine would have preferred to stay home.

  > If Jack had called two minutes sooner, Elaine wouldn't be in Japan right now.

  > If Jack were more responsible, he would think ahead.

(Use *were* with a singular subject after *if* or *as though*.)

Could, Can

Use *could* to refer to the past and *can* to refer to the present.

> *Past:* The engineer couldn't run the experiment because the ocean was too rough.

> *Present:* The engineer can not run the experiment because the ocean is too rough.

Use *could* to show what might happen and doesn't; use *can* to show ability.

> My parents make good money. They *could* buy us anything we want, but they don't.

> My parents make good money. They *can* buy us anything we want.

Gone, Eaten, Done, Seen, Written

Avoid expressions such as *I seen* and *He has went*. Use *gone, eaten, done, seen, written* after a helping verb.

We went.	We have gone.
I ate.	I have eaten.
He did it.	He has done it.
He saw the light.	He has seen the light.
She wrote for an hour.	She has written for an hour.

VERB AGREEMENT

The word before the verb is not always its subject. Look for *who* or *what* is doing the action.

- Remember that two singular subjects joined by *and* (for example, the bird and the bee) make a plural and need a plural verb.

    The bird and the bee make music together.
    My great aunt and my grandfather argue incessantly.

- Sometimes an insertion separates the subject and verb.

    The drummer, not the other musicians, sets the rhythm.

    Two causes for the collapse of their business were employee apathy and management dishonesty.

- Sometimes an *of* phrase separates the subject and verb; read the sentence without the *of* phrase.

    One of the guests was a sleepwalker.
    Each of us owns a Wurlitzer juke box.
    The use of cigarettes is dangerous.

- The subject of the sentence follows *there was, there were, there is, there are.*

    There was one reason for the cover-up.
    There were three reasons for the cover-up.

- Words with *one* and *body* are singular.

    Everyone except for the twins was laughing.
    Somebody always overheats the copying machine.

- Sometimes a group can be singular.

    My family does not eat crowder peas.
    In some states the jury elects the foreman.
    A thousand dollars is a lot of money to carry around.

- *-ing* phrases are usually singular.

    Dating two people is tricky.

Word Endings: *S* AND *ED*

If word endings give you problems, train yourself to check every noun to see if it needs *s* and every verb to see if it needs *s* or *ed*.

Add *ed*

- To form most simple past tenses

    She walked.   He tripped.   Mae asked a question.

- After *has, have, had*

    He has walked.   We have moved.   She had already arrived.

- After the *be* verbs (*are, were, is, was, am, be, been, being*)

    They are prejudiced against immigrants.
    She was depressed.
    Marge is engaged to be married.

Note that the *-ed* ending can sometimes appear in present and future tenses:

    They are supposed to leave on Friday.
    He will be prepared.

Do Not Add *ed*

- After *to*

    He loved to walk in the early morning.

- After *would, should, could*

    Sometimes she would work all night.
    Charles Atlas could lift two hundred pounds.

- After *did, didn't*

    Harpo didn't talk often.

- After an irregular past tense

    I bought bread.   She found her keys.
    The cup fell.   The shoes cost only seven dollars.

Add *s*

- To form a plural (more than one)

  many scientists   two potatoes   several families

- To the present tense of a verb that follows *he, she, it,* or a singular noun

  The system costs too much.   It appears every spring.

  She says what she thinks.   The dog sees the fire hydrant.

  Bill asks provocative questions. Polly insists on her rights.

Note: Usually when there is an *s* on the noun, there is no *s* on the verb.

  Pots rattle.   A pot rattles.
  The candles burn swiftly.   The candle burns swiftly.

- To form a possessive (with an apostrophe)

  John's mother   today's society
  Sally's house   women's clothing

Do Not Add *s* to a Verb

- If the subject of the sentence is plural

  Tulips come from Holland.
  Salt and sugar look the same.

- If one of these helping verbs comes before the main verb

  does   may   will   shall   can
  must   might   would   should   could

  Kenneth should clean out the back seat of his car.
  Angelica can get there in thirty minutes.
  The professor's attitude does make me angry.

For more help with word endings, see pages 10–11, 17, and 47.

TANGLED SENTENCES

Look at your sentences to make sure the parts go with each other.

■ PARALLEL STRUCTURE

The parts of a list (or pair) must be in the same format.

> *Not*
> *Parallel:* Lord Byron's travels took him to France,
> Switzerland, Italy, and to Greece

Here, two of the countries have *to* before them and two do not.
The word *to* must be used either before every item or before
only the first.

> *Correct:* Lord Byron's travels took him to France, to
> Switzerland, to Italy, and to Greece.

> *Correct:* Lord Byron's travels took him to France,
> Switzerland, Italy, and Greece.

> *Not*
> *Parallel:* To reach the camp, Marty paddled a canoe and
> then a horse.

Here, it sounds as if Marty paddled a horse.

> *Correct:* To reach the camp, Marty paddled a canoe and
> then rode a horse.

> *Not*
> *Parallel:* George Orwell hated his school because of the
> living conditions, the punishments, and the
> teachers only drilled facts into the students.

Here the first two parts of the list are nouns, but the third part is
a whole clause.

> *Correct:* George Orwell hated his school because the
> living conditions were disgusting, the
> punishments were cruel, and the teachers only
> drilled facts into the students.

■ DANGLERS

- There are two problems. In one, a word (often a pronoun) has been left out, so that the introductory phrase doesn't fit with what follows.

    Dangler: Dashing wildly across the platform, the train pulled out of the station.

    This sounds as if the subway dashed across the platform. To correct it, add the missing word or words.

    Correct: Dashing wildly across the platform, we saw the train pull out of the station.

    Correct: As we dashed wildly across the platform, the train pulled out of the station.

    Dangler: At the age of five, my mother took me to school for the first time.

    Technically, this sentence says that the mother was five.

    Correct: When I was five, my mother took me to school for the first time.

- The second problem occurs when a phrase or word in a sentence is too far from the part it goes with.

    Dangler: A former weight lifter, the reporter interviewed Terrence Harley about the use of steroids.

    This sounds as if the reporter is a former weightlifter.

    Correct: The reporter interviewed Terrence Harley, a former weight lifter, about the use of steroids.

■ MIXED SENTENCE PATTERNS

Sometimes you start with one way of getting to a point, but one of the words slides you into a different way of saying it. The two patterns get mixed up. Correct a mixed sentence by using one pattern or the other.

> *Mixed*
> *(incorrect):* By opening the window lets in fresh air.

Here the writer started to say "By opening the window, I let in fresh air," but the phrase *opening the window* took over.

> *Correct:*　By opening the window, I let in fresh air.
>
> *Correct:*　Opening the window lets in fresh air.

Read your sentence as a whole to make sure that the end goes with the beginning.

> *Mixed*
> *(incorrect):* In the Republic of Cameroon has more than two
> 　　　　　　　hundred local languages.
>
> *Correct:*　The Republic of Cameroon has more than two
> 　　　　　　　hundred local languages.
>
> *Correct:*　In the Republic of Cameroon, more than two
> 　　　　　　　hundred local languages are spoken.
>
> *Mixed*
> *(incorrect):* In "London," by William Blake presents a
> 　　　　　　　critique of the modern city.
>
> *Correct:*　In "London," William Blake presents a critique of
> 　　　　　　　the modern city.

Note that these problem sentences most often begin with *by* or *in.*

PART 2

PUTTING A PAPER TOGETHER

What to Do When You're Stuck

Sometimes the ideas don't seem to be there, or you have only two ideas, or your thoughts are disconnected and jumbled. Sometimes it's hard to know where to begin or what shape your writing should take.

Here are some techniques used by professional writers. Try several—some are better for particular kinds of writing. For instance, lists and outlines work when you don't have much time (in an essay exam) or when you have many points to include. Freewriting works well when your topic is subtle, when you want to write with depth. You'll find several techniques that work for you.

■ Techniques That Work

Break the Assignment into Easy Steps

You can take an intimidating assignment one step at a time. Start where you're most comfortable. Often, once you have some ideas written, one will lead to another, and you'll have a whole draft of your paper. Otherwise, by trying several of the following techniques, you may find that your paper is partly written and you have a clear sense of how to finish it.

Freewriting

In this method, you find your ideas by writing with no plan, quickly, without stopping. Don't worry about what to say first. Start somewhere in the middle. Just write nonstop for ten to twenty minutes. Ignore grammar, spelling, organization. Follow your thoughts as they come. Above all, don't stop! If you hit a blank place, write your last word over and over—you'll soon have a new idea. After you have freewritten several times, read what you've written and underline the good sentences. These can be the heart of your essay. Freewriting takes time, but it is the easiest way to begin and leads to surprising and creative results.

Lists and Outlines

With this method, before you write any sentences, you make a list of the points you might use in your essay, including any examples and details that come to mind. Jot them down briefly, a word or phrase for each item. Keeping these points brief makes them easier to read and rearrange. Include any ideas you think of in one long list down the page. When you run dry, wait a little—more ideas will come.

Now start grouping the items on the list. If you work on a computer, move related points together; if you are writing by hand, draw lines connecting examples to the points they illustrate. Then make a new list with the related points grouped together. Decide which idea is most important and cross out ideas or details that do not relate to it. Arrange your points so that each will lead up to the next. Be sure each section of your essay has examples or facts to strengthen your ideas.

You're ready to compose your paper. You'll see that this system works best when you have a big topic with many details. Although it seems complicated, it actually saves time. Once you have your plan, the writing of the essay will go very fast.

Writing a Short Draft First

In one page, write your ideas for the assignment, what you've thought of including. Take just ten or twenty minutes. Now you have a draft to work with. Expand each point with explanations or examples.

A similar technique is to write just one paragraph—at least six sentences—that tells the main ideas you have in mind. Arrange the sentences in a logical and effective sequence. Then copy each sentence from that core paragraph onto its own page and write a paragraph or two to back up each sentence. Now you have the rough draft of an essay. Remember, your first draft doesn't have to be perfect as long as it's good enough for you to work with.

Using a Tape Recorder

If you have trouble writing as fast as you think, talk your ideas into a recorder. Play them back several times, stopping to write down the best sentences. Another method is to write down four or five sentences before you begin, each starting with the main word of your topic, each different from the others. As you talk, use these sentences to get going when you run dry and to make sure you discuss different aspects of your topic.

Taking a Thirty-Minute Break

Go for a walk, listen to music, meditate, work out—whatever refreshes your mind without dulling it. Forget about your paper for half an hour.

Talking to a Friend

The idea here is for your friend to help you discover and organize *your* ideas—not to tell you his or her ideas. The best person for this technique is not necessarily a good writer but a good listener. Ask your friend just to listen and not say anything for a few minutes. As you talk, you should jot down points you make. Then ask what came across most vividly. As your friend responds, you may find yourself saying more, trying to make a point clearer. Make notes of the new points, but don't let your friend write or dictate words for you. Once you have plenty of notes, you're ready to be alone and to freewrite or outline.

■ TIME WASTERS: WHAT *NOT* TO DO

Don't Start Over Repeatedly

Keep going straight ahead. Write a complete first draft before making major revisions. When an idea comes to you out of sequence, jot it on a separate page.

Don't Use a Dictionary or Thesaurus before the Second Draft

Delay your concern for precise word usage and spelling until you have the whole paper written. Then go back and make improvements.

Don't Spend Hours on an Outline

You will probably revise your outline after the first draft, so don't get bogged down at the beginning. Even with long papers, a topic outline (naming the idea for each paragraph without supporting details) is often an efficient way to organize.

Don't Try to Make Only One Draft

You may think you can save time by writing only one draft, but you can't get everything perfect the first time. Actually, it's faster to write something *approximately* close to the points you want to make, then go back and revise.

Don't Write with Distractions

When you write, you need to focus your physical and mental energy. You can be distracted by music, television, or conversation in the background or by being too uncomfortable or too comfortable. You may not even realize how much these distractions can diffuse your energy and concentration.

ADDRESSING YOUR AUDIENCE

Before you get very far into writing anything, stop and ask yourself: Who is going to read this? Considering your audience will guide you in several crucial decisions.

Tone Decide how formal or informal you should be.

* Can you be playful or should you be straightforward and serious?

* Should you include personal experiences?

* Can you use *I*? *I* is usually preferable—it is more direct and more graceful than avoiding *I*—but you do not have to keep saying *I think* or *In my opinion.*

For most audiences, avoid being cute, sarcastic, or slangy; but also avoid being stiff and artificial.

Level of Information Think about what your audience already knows about this topic.

* What can you skip or sum up quickly?

* What must you explain?

You will need to explain points or terms your audience may not be familiar with. But you must be careful not to fill your paper with tedious information most people already know.

Persuasion Consider your audience's assumptions about the subject and about the position you plan to take.

* What opening will engage their interest?

* Which arguments, which evidence will best make your case for this specific audience?

Think about concerns and opinions your audience may already have about the subject you are presenting. Anticipate their questions and arguments. Answer the questions you feel certain they will have and find strong counterarguments to support your own position.

The Teacher as Audience

You write best if you write with authority—if you know what you're talking about. In an essay based on personal experience, you are the authority since you are the one who lived it. In many research papers, you may come to know more about the topic than your teacher does.

But in most college writing, the teacher is the authority—if not on your specific topic, at least on the writing requirements for the course. Overcome feeling intimidated, which leads to merely trying to guess what the teacher wants. Instead, look for issues that are real to you, aspects of the subject that connect to ideas you've considered in the past, aspects of the subject that you respond to strongly. Articulate these ideas and responses, but present them in a way that will share them with your teacher and that build on what you have learned in class.

In some writing classes, your audience also includes your classmates. You can imagine yourself reading your paper aloud to a group of them. Imagining faces as you write can inspire you to say what you most care about.

Writing in Your Profession

For a business or other professional audience, there are additional requirements to consider. Above all, don't waste your reader's time!

- Put the main point up front and highlight the important facts.

- Be very direct and clear—rather than subtly building up to your point.

- Use professional terminology when necessary, but avoid any unnecessary jargon.

- Avoid lengthy examples.

One caution: you don't know who will end up reading a letter or report. E-mails get forwarded and circulated. Bear in mind the secondary audience—in some cases, your writing could even become evidence in a court of law.

When you don't have a clear sense of your audience, imagine people in front of you (make it a large group) and then have that audience ask you questions. Answer their questions on paper and you will be aiming your essay right at a general audience—the audience most pieces are written for.

WRITING IN CLASS

A wave of panic—that's what most people feel when they are handed an assignment to be written in class. Some students, feeling the pressure, plunge in and write the first thoughts that come to mind. But your first thoughts aren't necessarily your best thoughts. There's a smarter way to write in a limited time.

Take Your Time at the Beginning

- Reread the instructions carefully. Be sure you're writing what you've been asked for.

- Jot down brief notes for a few minutes. Don't write whole sentences yet—just a word or phrase for each idea, example, or fact.

- Take a few more minutes to expand your notes. Stay calm. Don't start writing too soon.

- Decide on the parts of your essay.

For an Essay about Information, Stress Your Organization

- Write an introduction that indicates the parts of your essay. One simple technique is to give a full sentence in your introduction for each of the main points you plan to make:

  > Sigmund Freud is famous for three important ideas. He popularized the idea that we repress or bottle up our feelings. He explored the idea of the unconscious. Most important, he stressed the idea that our family relationships when we are children determine our adult relationships.

  Note how the number "three" in the first sentence helps the reader to see the plan of the whole essay.

- Write a paragraph for each point using the same order as you did in your introduction. In each middle paragraph, restate the point, explain what you mean by any general words, and give facts or examples to prove your point.

- Write a brief conclusion, stressing what's most important.

- For *short essays on an exam,* each answer should consist of one long paragraph. Write a one-sentence introduction that uses words from the question and asserts your answer. Then, in the same paragraph, present three facts to support your answer, explaining one fact at a time. Finally, sum up your position in the last sentence of the paragraph.

For a Personal Essay, Stress What You Have Discovered

While the three-point essay can get you by, it can easily become stilted and boring. In a personal essay, you have many more options.

- If you're asked to write about a significant event in your life, begin your essay by describing it *briefly.* Use vivid details to bring it to life. Then use most of your essay to tell what you learned from this event or how it has changed you. Remember to divide your essay into paragraphs.

- If you're asked to give your opinion about a topic, you sometimes can use personal examples to support your position. In your introduction make clear where you stand. Then give each important point its own paragraph with examples. Use your own experiences, your own observations, and incidents you've read about.

- If you can't come up with a strong introduction at first, go ahead and write your essay. In the process you might discover a central idea that can then serve as your introduction.

- In your conclusion, don't preach and don't fall back on overused generalizations. Say what matters to you or what you have discovered.

STRATEGIES TO SAVE TIME

Don't Start Over

- Stick to your plan. If you get a new idea, use an asterisk (*) or an arrow to show where it goes.

- Leave room after each paragraph for ideas you might want to add later. If you are writing in an exam booklet, write on only the front side of the page so that you will have room for insertions.

- If you add or cut a main point, go back and revise your introduction to match the change.

Don't Pad Your Writing

Use a direct, no-nonsense style. Don't try for big words—they just lead to errors when you are under time pressure. Simply state your points and the facts to back them up, one step at a time.

Don't Make a Neat Copy

Copying over wastes precious time, and the copy tends to be full of slips and errors. Instead, put a line through an error and correct it above the line; use a caret (^) for a short insertion, an asterisk (*) or arrow for a long insertion.

Don't Rush at the End

- Stop writing ten minutes before the end of the allotted time.

- Read your essay for content. Don't add to it unless you find a *major* omission. Late additions usually create errors and disorganization.

- Proofread, with special attention to the second half of the essay (where rushing leads to errors) and to the very first sentence. Look closely for the errors you usually make. Look for words like *to* and *too, then* and *than.* Check your *periods* to be sure you have no run-on sentences or fragments. Look carefully to make sure that you haven't left out any words or letters.

Finding an Organization for Your Essay

Your goal in organizing is to produce a sequence of paragraphs that leads the reader to a single strong conclusion. But there are many ways to reach this goal.

Some people need an outline; others write first and then reorganize when they see a pattern in their writing. Still others begin in the middle or write the parts of their papers out of order.

No method is the "right" one. Some approaches are better for certain topics; some are better for certain people. Do not feel that you have to fit into a set way of working.

Using a Formula as a Plan

Sometimes a teacher will give you a specific format to follow, but most of the time you will need to discover the organization that best enhances the content of your essay. A formula is especially useful for assignments you must do repeatedly or quickly. For instance, lab reports usually follow a set format: (1) Question to be Investigated; (2) The Experiment; (3) Observations; (4) Conclusions. Some topics lend themselves to particular arrangements. Here are a few:

Common Patterns of Organization

chronological (the sequence in which events occurred)
narrative (how you learned what you know)
generalization, followed by examples or arguments
process (the steps for how something is done)
comparison (similarities and differences)
classification (types and categories)
problem and solution
cause and effect (or a result and its causes)
a brief case study or story, followed by interpretation of what it shows
dramatic order (building to the strongest point)

If what you want to say fits one of these patterns, you can organize your paper efficiently. However, formulas quite often create boring papers. For most topics you will need to discover the best plan by making lists of ideas and reordering them, or by writing for a while and then reworking what you've written.

Creating a Rough Outline

Here's a method that works for many writers:

- Make a random list—written in *phrases,* not sentences—of all the ideas and facts you want to include. Don't be stingy. Make a long list.

- Now look at your list and decide which are your main points and which points support them.

- Write a single sentence or two that contain the major point you are going to make. Make sure that this point is stated early in your essay.

- Decide on the order of your main points.

- Delete points from your list that do not fit the pattern or plan you are using. Remember, you can't put in everything you know.

- Decide on your paragraphs; write a sentence for each paragraph that tells what you plan to say.

- Now write a rough draft before you reconsider your organization.

When to Adjust Your Plan

Sometimes the trick to good organization is *reorganization.* No matter whether you start with an outline, no matter what you think when you begin, your topic may well shift and change as you write. Often you will come up with better ideas, and as a result, you may change your emphasis. Therefore, you must be ready to abandon parts or all of your original plan. Some minor points may now become major points. Most writers need to revise their plan *after* they finish a first draft.

Here are the signs that a paper needs to be reorganized:

- Parts of the paper are boring.

- Your real point doesn't show up until the end.

- You have repeated the same idea in several different places.

- The essay seems choppy and hard to follow.

- Your paragraphs are either too short or too long.

In the end, make sure that you know the main point you want the reader to get and that every sentence contributes to making that point clear.

INTRODUCTIONS

Beginnings demand special attention. An introduction should snag your reader's interest. Pretend that you are a reader leafing through a magazine: what opening would make you stop and read an article on your topic?

Sometimes you may get stuck writing an introduction. In that case, try writing your introduction *after* you've written the rest of the first draft. Often you don't find your real main point until you've written several pages. However, in an essay exam or under time pressure, write the introduction first to indicate the map of the paper.

Here are a few common methods for beginning an essay:

Indicate the Parts of Your Essay

In many academic papers and in technical or business reports, the introduction should indicate what is coming. Write a brief paragraph summing up the points you plan to make, one at a time. Then, in the middle of your paper, develop each point into one or more paragraphs.

> Three factors caused the sudden population increase in eighteenth-century Europe. First, the newly settled colonies provided enough wealth to support more people. Second, eighteenth-century wars did not kill as many Europeans as did seventeenth-century wars. Finally, the discovery of the potato provided a cheap food source.

Sometimes you can indicate the parts of your essay more subtly:

> Although *Walden* and *Adventures of Huckleberry Finn* treat similar themes, the two books have very different tones and implications.

Take a Bold Stand

Start out with a strong statement of your position.

> Millard Filmore is the most underrated President in American history.

Start with the Other Side

Tell what you disagree with and who said it. Give the opposing reasons so that you can later prove them wrong. For examples of this technique, see the editorial or "opinion" page of your newspaper.

Tell a Brief Story

Give one or two paragraphs to a single typical case, and then make your general point. The brief story can catch the reader's interest and make clear the personal implications of the topic you will present.

Use the News Lead

Write one sentence incorporating *who, what, when, where, how,* and sometimes *why.*

> During the fourteenth century, in less than three years, one-third of Europe's population died of the bubonic plague.

Move from the General to the Specific

Begin with the wider context of the topic and then zero in on the case at hand.

> When we think of "strength," we usually picture physical strength—for instance, a weight lifter. But there are subtler forms of strength. Perhaps the rarest is moral strength: the ability to do what is right, even when it is inconvenient, unpopular, or dangerous. My grandfather in Italy was actually a strongman in the circus, but I remember him for his moral strength rather than for his powerful arms.

Paragraphs—Long and Short

The paragraphs of your essay lead the reader step by step through your ideas. Each paragraph should make one point, and every sentence in it should relate to that one point. Usually the paragraph begins by stating the point and then goes on to explain it and make it specific.

Paragraphs should be as long as they need to be to make one point. On occasion, one or two strong sentences can be enough. At other times you need nine or ten sentences to explain your point. However, you want to avoid writing an essay that consists of either one long paragraph or a series of very short ones. Paragraphs give readers a visual landing, a place to pause; so use your eye and vary the lengths of your paragraphs.

■ Indent the First Line of the Paragraph

In college papers, indent the first line of each paragraph half an inch. In business letters or reports, where you single-space between lines, omit the indentation and double-space between the paragraphs to divide them.

■ Break Up Long Paragraphs

A paragraph that is more than ten sentences usually should be divided. Find a natural point for division, such as

- A new subject or idea

- A turning point in a story

- The start of an example

- A change of location or time

■ EXPAND SHORT PARAGRAPHS

Too many short paragraphs can make your thought seem fragmented. If you have a string of paragraphs that consist of one or two sentences, you may need to *combine, develop,* or *omit* some of your paragraphs.

Combine

- Join two paragraphs on the same point.

- Include examples in the same paragraph as the point they illustrate.

- Regroup your major ideas and make a new paragraph plan.

Develop

- Give examples or reasons to support your point.

- Cite facts, statistics, or evidence to support your point.

- Relate an incident or event that supports your point.

- Explain any important general terms.

- Quote authorities to back up what you say.

Omit

If you have a short paragraph that cannot be expanded or combined with another, chances are that paragraph should be dropped. Sometimes you have to decide whether you really want to explain a particular point or whether it's not important to your paper.

■ CHECK FOR CONTINUITY

Within a paragraph, make sure that your sentences follow a logical sequence. Each one should build on the previous one and lead to the next.

Link your paragraphs together with transitions—taking words or ideas from one paragraph and using them at the beginning of the next one.

■ A Tip

If you keep having trouble with your paragraphs, you can rely on this basic paragraph pattern:

- A main point stated in one sentence
- An explanation of any general words in your main point
- Examples or details that support your point
- The reason each example supports your point
- A sentence to sum up

TRANSITIONS

Transitions are *bridges* in your writing that take the reader from one thought to the next. These bridges link your ideas and help you to avoid choppy writing. You need transitions between paragraphs that show the movement from one idea to the next, and you also need transitions to connect sentences within a paragraph.

First Check the Order of Your Ideas

If you are having trouble with transitions, it may be that your points are out of order. Make a list of your points and juggle the order so that one point leads logically to the next. Then add transitions that underscore the movement from one point to the other.

Use Transition Words

Keep your transitions brief and inconspicuous. Here are some choices of transition words you can use to illustrate certain points or relationships:

Adding a point:	furthermore, besides, finally, in addition to
Emphasis:	above all, indeed, in fact, in other words, most important
Time:	then, afterward, eventually, next, immediately, meanwhile, previously, already, often, since then, now, later, usually
Space:	next to, across, from, above, below, nearby, inside, beyond, between, surrounding
Cause and effect:	consequently, as a result, therefore, thus
Examples:	for example, for instance
Progression:	first, second, third, furthermore
Contrast:	but, however, in contrast, instead, nevertheless, on the other hand, though, still, unfortunately
Similarity:	like, also, likewise, similarly, as, then too

Concession: although, yet, of course, after all, granted, while it is true

Conclusions: therefore, to sum up, in brief, in general, in short, for these reasons, in retrospect, finally, in conclusion

Use Repetition of Key Words

- Repeat the word itself or variations of it.

    I can never forget the *year* of the flood. That was the *year* I grew up.

    Everyone agreed that Adlai Stevenson was *intelligent.* His *intelligence,* however, did not always endear him to the voters.

- Use pronouns.

    People who have hypoglycemia usually need to be on a special diet. *They* should, at the very least, avoid eating sugar.

- Use synonyms—different words with the same meaning.

    When you repot plants, be certain to use a high grade of potting *soil.* Plants need good rich *dirt* in order to thrive.

    Even though the woman was *handcuffed,* she kept running around, waving her *manacled* hands in the air.

Use Transitional Sentences to Link Paragraphs

Usually the transition between paragraphs comes in the first sentence of the new paragraph.

    Even though Hortense followed all of these useful suggestions, she still ran into an unforeseen problem.

    Because of these results, the researchers decided to try a new experiment.

Notice that, in these examples, the first half of the sentence refers to a previous paragraph; the second half points to the paragraph that is beginning.

CONCLUSIONS

Don't end your paper with preaching or clichés. Consider, out of all that you have written, what is most important. Sometimes you want a quick summation, but other times you will have a longer conclusion that probes your topic more deeply.

To get a memorable last sentence, try writing five sentences. They can express the same basic idea, but they should be worded as differently as possible—one long, one short, one plain, one elegant. If you write five, you'll find the one you want.

Here are several approaches to writing a conclusion:

Return to Your Introduction

Look back at the issues you raised in your introduction. Using some of the same language, say what your essay has added to your initial thoughts. The point is not to repeat your introduction but to build on it.

Summarize

Stress your main points, but avoid repeating earlier phrases word for word. Summaries can be boring, so make an effort to give yours some kick.

Suggest a Solution to a Problem

Come up with a solution you think might make a difference, and tell how your findings could affect the future.

Put Your Ideas in a Wider Perspective

What is the importance of what you have said? What is the larger meaning? Move from the specifics of your topic to the deeper concerns it suggests.

Raise Further Questions or Implications

Which issues now remain? Acknowledge the limitations of what you have covered. Reaffirm what you *have* established. Examine what it implies.

Above all, don't just limp out of your paper. Leave your reader with a strong and memorable statement.

How to Make a Paper Longer (and When to Make It Shorter)

Adding words and phrases to your paper makes it at most an inch longer. Adding new points or new examples will make it grow half a page at a time. On the other hand, there are times when cutting a little bit will make your whole paper stronger.

How to Make a Paper Longer

- Add an example or explain your reasons to clarify your point—or even add a new point.

- Mention other views of the subject that differ from yours: either incorporate them (showing the evidence for them) or disprove them (telling why others might accept them and why you reject them).

- Add details (facts, events that happened, things you can see or hear). Details are the life of a paper. Instead of writing, "We got something to drink," write "We took water from the stream with Stacey's tin cup. The water was so cold it hurt our stomachs."

- Expand your conclusion: Discuss implications and questions that your paper brings to mind.

but

- Don't add empty phrases, because they make your writing boring. Don't fake length by using fat margins, big handwriting, or a large typeface.

When to Make a Paper Shorter

- Condense minor points. Sometimes you think a point is necessary, but when you read your paper to a friend, you notice that you both get bored in that section. Or sometimes you get tangled up trying to make a point clear when you can cover it briefly or cut it entirely.

- Watch your *pace* when you tell a series of events. Head toward the main point or event directly. Don't get lost in boring preliminary details.

- Avoid getting sidetracked. The digression may interest you, but it may not add to the real point of the essay.

- Check to see if you have repeated any point several times. If so, decide on the most effective place to make that point and make it fully in one place.

How to Work on a Second Draft

Computers make revision easier, but it's not enough simply to patch up a first draft by inserting a phrase or sentence in a few spots or by merely spellchecking. Revision is not just fixing errors. It means taking a fresh look at your paper. You may need to move some parts of it, add the details of a point you have barely mentioned, or completely rewrite a section.

This chapter offers you a number of ways to improve your paper.

What Is the Real Goal of Your Paper?

- A big danger is straying from your subject. It's tempting to include good ideas or long examples that are related to your subject but do not support your main point.

- Your *real* point may not be the point with which you started. Decide what you are really saying. You may need to write a new introduction that stresses your real goal.

- You might find it helpful to write a note to yourself that begins, "The main point of my paper is . . . " Keep it in front of you as you revise.

The Order of Your Points

Reconsider the organization of your ideas.

- Make a list of your points in the order you wrote them.

- Now play with the order so that each one logically leads to the next.

- Get rid of points that aren't related.

- Cover some points briefly as parts of other points.

- Help your reader to navigate through your paper by making a logical transition to each new idea.

Strong Parts and Weak Parts

- Build up what's good. When revising, writers tend to focus on the weak spots. Instead, start by looking for the good parts in your paper. Underline or highlight them, and write more about them. Add examples. Explain more fully. You may find that you have written a new, much better paper.

- Fix up what's bad. Now look at the parts that are giving you trouble. Do you really need them? Are they in the right place? If you got tangled up trying to say something that you consider important, stop and ask yourself, "What is it I'm trying to say, after all?" Then say it to yourself in plain English and write it down that way.

Give the Reader the Picture

Make sure the reader really sees what you mean.

- If you are telling a story, put in the strong details that convey what the experience was like.

- If you are arguing for a position, fully explain your reasons and lay out the evidence.

- If you are expressing an opinion, tell specifically what gave you that idea.

Get Help at the Writing Center

Your college writing center is staffed by professionals trained to assist you with your writing. Bring your paper, and a tutor will give you constructive advice. You also may be able to get help from the writing center online.

Read Aloud to a Friend

- When you read your paper to a friend, notice what you *add* as you read—what information or explanations you feel compelled to put in. Jot down these additions and put them into the paper.

- Ask your friend to tell you what came through. All you want is what he or she heard—not whether it's good, not how to change it. Then let your friend ask you questions. However, don't let your friend take over and tell you what to write.

Final Touches

- Look again at the proportions of your paper. Are some of the paragraphs too short and choppy? Is there one that is overly long?

- Look at your introduction and conclusion. Play with the first and last sentences of your paper in order to begin and end with the strongest statements that you can. Write the idea three or four different ways—with very different wording—then choose the best.

- Write a title that catches the reader's attention and announces your specific subject.

- Be sure to use the spellcheck to catch trouble spots. Then proofread your paper closely several times, watching especially for errors in any of the new material you've written.

PROOFREADING TIPS

The key to proofreading is doing it several times. Careless errors undermine what you have said, so make a practice of proofreading methodically.

Here are some tips to help you spot mistakes.

Make a Break between Writing and Proofreading

Always put a little distance between the writing of a paper and the proofreading of it. That way you'll see it fresh and catch errors you might have otherwise overlooked. Set the paper aside for the night—or even for twenty minutes—while you catch your breath. When you write in class, train yourself *not* to write up until the final moment; give yourself an extra ten minutes before the end of class to proofread your paper several times before handing it in.

Search for Trouble

Assume that you have made unconscious errors and really look for them. Slow down your reading considerably, and actually look at every word.

Know Your Own Typical Mistakes

Before you proofread, look over any papers you've already gotten back corrected. Recall the errors you need to watch for. As you're writing *this* paper, take ten minutes to learn from the last one.

Proofread for One Type of Error

If periods and commas are your biggest problem, or if you always leave off apostrophes, or if you always write *your* for *you're,* go through the paper checking for just that one problem. Then go back and proofread to check for other mistakes.

Proofread Out of Order

Try starting with the last sentence of the paper and reading backwards to the first sentence; or proofread the second half of the paper first (since that's where most of the errors usually are), take a break, and then proofread the first half.

Proofread Aloud

Always try to read your paper aloud at least once. This will slow you down, and you'll *hear* the difference between what you meant to write and what you actually wrote.

Look Up Anything You're Not Sure Of

Use this book and a dictionary. You'll learn nothing by guessing, but you'll learn something forever if you take the time to look it up.

With a Computer, Proofread on Both Screen and Page

Scroll through and make corrections on the screen. Double-check places where you have inserted or deleted material. Use the spellcheck, but remember that it will not catch commonly confused words like *to* and *too* or *your* and *you're*.

Proofread Your Final Copy Several Times

It does no good to proofread a draft of your paper and then forget to proofread the final copy. This problem crops up often, especially in typewritten papers. Remember: A *typo* is just as much an error as any other error.

FORMAT OF COLLEGE PAPERS

The following guidelines are appropriate for most college papers. Ask your teacher for any specific requirements.

■ TYPING YOUR PAPER

Typeface

- Use a 12-point typeface on the computer.
- Do not use all capital letters, all italics, all boldface, or strange fonts.

Spacing

- Set your computer to double-space between lines; you should get approximately twenty-seven lines per page. (Double-space even for long quotations.)
- Use a one-inch margin on all four sides.
- Indicate the beginning of each paragraph either by indenting the first line five spaces or by skipping a line and starting at the left margin (block format). Do not mix these methods.
- Do not justify (line up the margin) on the right unless asked to do so. Justifying on the right distorts the spacing between letters and words, making your paper harder to read.
- At the bottom of the page, use a full last line, unless you're ending a paragraph. It's all right to end a page in mid-sentence.

Spacing after Punctuation

- Leave one space after most punctuation marks.

Periods	Commas	Colons
Semicolons	Question marks	Exclamation marks

  Your teacher may prefer the older convention of two spaces after a sentence.

- Make a dash by using two hyphens--with no space before or after.

- Make an ellipsis (. . .) by using three periods with a space before and after each period.

- Never begin a line with a period or a comma.

- Never put a space before a punctuation mark (except for an ellipsis or an opening parenthesis).

Dividing Words When Writing by Hand

- Avoid, as much as possible, dividing a word from one line to the next. If you can, fit it on one line or the other.

- If you must divide a very long word, divide only between syllables. To find the syllables, look up the word in a dictionary. It will be printed with dots between the syllables: *ex • per • i • men • ta • tion.*

- Never divide a one-syllable word, like *brought*. Never divide a word after only one letter.

Header with Page Number

Create a header with your last name and the page number on each page after the first.

■ ASSEMBLING YOUR PAPER

Cover Sheet or First Page

Include

- The title, without quotation marks or underlining

- Your name

- The course title and number

- The teacher's name

- The date

If you use a cover sheet, center the title in the middle of the page, and put the other information in the lower right-hand corner. If you don't use a cover sheet, put your name and so forth in the upper-left corner; then skip two lines and center the title.

Binding

- Staple once or clip in the upper-left corner.

- Do not put your paper in a binder or folder unless you have been asked to.

■ SUBMITTING PAPERS ELECTRONICALLY

When you submit a paper electronically,

- Single space and use block format for paragraphs (no initial indent).

- Skip a line between paragraphs, and number your paragraphs (put the numbers in brackets).

- Either use one underline before and after a title you normally would underline, or italicize when using HTML.

- Save as a text or HTML file.

■ A WORD ABOUT PROOFREADING

- A typo counts as an error; it's no excuse to say, "Oh, that's just a typo."

- Proofread your paper both on the monitor and on the hard copy. Don't rely solely on a spellcheck; it will miss errors like *to* for *too*.

- If necessary, make last-minute corrections with a pen: Draw a line through the word you wish to change and write the correction above the line.

PART 3

THE RESEARCH PAPER

How to Start a Research Project

Here it comes again, that terrifying request from a teacher for a "research" or "term" paper. You don't have to be scared by the names of these papers. A research or term paper is simply a fairly long paper in which you set forth a point of view and support it with outside sources of information.

The trouble with many student papers is that they present information one source at a time, pretty much copying from the sources and changing a few words. Instead, a good research paper presents *your* view of the topic, guiding the reader one idea at a time into what you have come to understand. Even in an "objective" research paper, you are your reader's guide to the subject.

■ Write First, Research Second

To conduct efficient research, you have to know what you're looking for. If you connect right away to the Web or head straight to the library, you're likely to waste your time by wandering around in a maze of information, jumping for the first book or website you find, or changing from subtopic to subtopic.

One hour spent defining your goals can save you many hours in the long run.

Freewrite about the Topic

To discover your preliminary focus, take fifteen minutes to write down the reasons you're interested in this subject, what you already know about it, and questions you'd like to answer.

List Your Research Questions

What do you hope to find out through research? List all the questions that you want to answer, and mark the ones that have the highest priority.

Narrow Your Topic

Before searching for reading materials, limit what you'll attempt to cover; otherwise, you will read yourself into a hole and never get your paper written. One method is to write a controlling sentence (a *thesis statement* or *topic sentence*) that will explain and limit your paper. You may sometimes have to use two sentences, but try for one.

> Pizza is the most wholesome fast food on the American market today.

In this example, the general topic of "pizza" has been narrowed to a focus on the nutritional value of pizza.

■ START WITH A REFERENCE BOOK

If a topic is very new to you, start with an introduction to the subject in a textbook or encyclopedia. For instance, if you have chosen to write about the nutritional value of pizza, you'd be wise to read up on nutritional guidelines in general.

■ COLLECT SEARCH TERMS

Search terms are words and phrases that you can use to find materials on your topic. For example, information on pizza can be found with the search terms

fast food	Italian cookery	pizza
mozzarella	Domino's	Pizza Hut

You will need a list of search terms whether you are using the Internet, a library catalog, a computerized database, or a printed index. Make a list of the key words in your subject— different ways it can be called, categories it fits into, and subtopics. Add to your list by reviewing class notes, looking in a textbook, browsing on the Web, or reading an encyclopedia article. Names of authors and other experts in the field can be good search terms.

■ USE A VARIETY OF SOURCES

Don't limit your research by sticking only to the sources you're most comfortable with. You might find it easy to search the Internet and difficult to go to the library. Or you might know how to find a book in the library but not how to find articles in periodicals. Or you might enjoy getting articles from magazines at home but don't like reading newspapers on microfilm. Use your ingenuity to come up with a variety of sources and to track down leads.

Network. Tell your family and friends that you're looking for information; ask them to save articles for you and to listen for reports on the radio or television.

Ask an expert. A teacher, businessperson, physician, or other expert on the subject can point you to the most valuable sources. You might even make an appointment to tape an interview and get the real lowdown on the topic from an expert.

Look for unusual sources outside of the library. Many valuable resources can be found both in and near your home. For example:

- Use the telephone book to find organizations devoted to your topic.

- Visit a business, a museum, or another institution.

- Rent a documentary videotape.

- Call a relevant government office.

■ MANAGE YOUR TIME

A major decision all researchers face is gauging how much time to allow for research and how much time to allow for writing the finished paper. Writing the paper itself will almost always take much longer than you expect.

These three tricks of the trade will save you from falling into a bottomless research hole:

Expect delays. Leave a margin of time for small disasters—books missing from the library, Internet meltdowns, or computer freezes.

Write parts of your paper as you go along. Don't just save a good idea in your head; it will float away.

Know when to stop your research. Set a deadline for when you'll stop looking for more information.

Three Essential Research Skills

Whether you're conducting research in the library or at home on your computer, you'll need these skills to find good sources of information and to extract what you need from them:

- Using search terms
- Choosing the best sources
- Taking usable notes

▓ Using Search Terms

Single Search Terms

For many listings, you can look under only one term at a time; therefore, you will need to try several of your search terms. In your search, remember to

- Use synonyms for different search terms.
- Narrow down the subject several times.

Searching through Menus

Often during electronic searches you will see a list of topics; click on one and you will see a list of subtopics; click on one and you'll see sub-subtopics; and so forth. This method is good for a start, but it is not as precise as combining search terms.

Combining Search Terms

In many electronic formats, you can and should use combinations of different search terms. Let's say you're interested in the nutritional value of pizza. You can combine the term *pizza* with terms like *nutrition, health, calories,* and *fat.*

Every search program uses slightly different rules of operation, but most use two searching conventions:

- Quotation marks to indicate that a phrase is to be treated as one search term—"fast food"

- Boolean operators:

  and specifies that both terms should appear

  > pizza and nutrition

  or specifies that either term should appear

  > pepperoni or sausage

  not specifies that a term should not appear

  > domino's not game

When a search program says that "Boolean *and* is implied," you don't need to type *and;* just type in all the terms you want with a space between them.

> pizza nutrition calorie fat

Some search programs use the plus (+) sign to mean that a particular term must appear, and the minus sign (–) instead of *not.*

> +pizza+sausage–pepperoni

As you narrow the focus of your research, keep adjusting your combination of search terms.

WHEN YOU FIND TOO FEW OR TOO MANY SOURCES

The help line for the particular program you are using is your first resource when you're in a jam. Here are some other steps to take:

No Match for Your Request

- You may have misspelled one or more words.
- You may have used the wrong symbols or phrasing for that particular search engine.
- You may have submitted too narrow a search. Try generalizing a bit—for example change the phrase "fat

content of pizza" to "fat and pizza," or add alternatives ("nonfat or lowfat").

- Give both the abbreviation and the full name, linked by *or* ("NIH or National Institutes of Health").

- You may need to try a different search engine or database.

- The information may be there, but your computer cannot reach it at this time. Try later.

Too Many Listings

- Take a look at the first ten results to see if they coincide at all with your topic. For instance, if your inquiry on pizza yielded thousands of articles, and the first ten are all about specific restaurants, you'll need to rephrase the search.

- If the first ten listings are on your topic, skim a few of them to extract more search terms.

- Add more words to your search string.

    pizza+calorie+carbohydrate+protein+fat

- Try putting a more specific word first in a search string.

- Use *not* or the minus sign (–) in front of terms that you do not want.

    pizza not restaurant not parlor not delivery

    pizza–restaurant–parlor–delivery

■ CHOOSING THE BEST SOURCES OF INFORMATION

Search first for information electronically when you can. Use the library's online catalog to find books and media materials on your subject. Use CD-ROM indexes to find articles in periodicals, journals, magazines, and newspapers. Ask the librarian for specialized databases in your subject field. On the Internet, use several search engines, subject directories, and reference pages. See pages 168–70, below.

All books and articles are not equal. Some are too old or too specialized or too superficial for your purposes. Others are not really relevant to your specific angle on the topic. Be prepared to reject sources that don't fit your topic. Look for a mix of books and articles, making sure that most of your sources are up-to-date, especially for scientific and technical topics. (For literary and historical topics, some older books are superior.)

Consider the level of information you require. A twenty-page paper needs much more detailed information and analysis than a five-page paper. A paper on the nutritional value of fast foods will be much more complex for a class in nutrition than for English 101.

Stick to your angle on the topic. As you look through the sources you've gathered, focus on the primary questions you've set out to answer. Don't let a source on a different subtopic lead you away from your goals. One skill of a good researcher is knowing which books and articles to bypass.

Consult the "List of Valuable Sources" at the back of this book. You will find a variety of electronic and print sources of information.

■ TAKING USABLE NOTES

Good notes are brief—you don't want to copy or download large chunks of information. Nor can you write your paper while taking notes. Taking notes and writing your paper must be two separate steps.

Record Bibliographical Information

Make sure you have the details about your source that you will need for your *Works Cited, References,* or *Bibliography.*

For a book: author, title, place of publication, publisher, and date of publication.

For an article: author, title of article, title of publication, date, and pages.

For an article on the Internet: author (if given), title of article (or type of article if e-mail or posting to a bulletin board), complete Internet address, and date you viewed it. Some programs will automatically record this for you—others won't.

Keep Your Notes Brief but Understandable

Next, take notes *sparingly* as you read. Take notes in phrases, not whole sentences. You will run yourself crazy if you try to take down every word, and your notes will be harder for you to read. If a quotation strikes you as well said or interesting, copy it word for word and put quotation marks around it in your notes.

Copying to Your Disk or Photocopying

Copying is a real time saver, but it increases the risk of plagiarism. Use a separate file for each item copied electronically. The point is to remember that *every word of downloaded material is copied (plagiarized)*. This material cannot be used honestly in your own paper *as is* but must be carefully quoted from, paraphrased, or summarized. Of course, you will be able to see that a photocopy is not your own writing, but you still must be able to tell where it came from; so immediately write the publication information on the photocopy.

In any case, a photocopy or a copy to your disk is not a substitute for notes. When you take notes, you are taking a step toward putting the information you've found into your own words.

Flashes of Insight

If you get an insight of your own as you are reading, stop and write about it. You may suddenly think of a great opening line, or realize that your points should come in a certain order, or disagree strongly with what you are reading. These ideas will evaporate if you don't take a minute to write them down immediately.

Getting Information at the Library

The library is your best single source of information. Under one roof, you can find a vast array of print material that goes back for years, plus a wide variety of electronic sources of information, including connections to the Internet.

The danger in the library is not knowing what you want and therefore getting lost in the maze of research. To avoid getting lost, be sure to write down in advance the primary questions you hope to answer and search terms you can use in your research.

■ Finding a Book

Your first step in finding a book is to search in the online catalog.

Books, media holdings, and reference materials are cataloged by author, title, and subject. At least in the beginning, you will be using the subject catalog to locate books and authors. On the computer, follow the system's instructions to see a "brief display," listing several books, or to see a "full display," giving detailed information about each book. Use a variety of general search terms. For example, you probably won't find a book entitled *The Nutritional Value of Pizza*, but you will find books including both of the subjects *pizza* and *nutrition*.

When you find books that look valuable, copy down the catalog numbers you need, or have the computer print a list for you. You need the complete call number in order to locate a book. It also helps to copy down the author and title. Once you find the book on the shelf, take time to browse through that section for other relevant titles.

■ FINDING AN ARTICLE

Articles in magazines, newspapers, and scholarly journals have information that is more up-to-date than books and thus provide an essential resource for good research.

Reference Section

Most teachers do not consider encyclopedia and dictionary articles adequate sources for college research papers. Nevertheless, encyclopedias and specialized reference books are often the best place to start your research because they give you an overview of your subject. The reference section of the library also contains dictionaries, bibliographies, and special collections of statistical information. You should ask the librarian where to browse for your particular subject.

Periodical Indexes and Databases

To find articles in newspapers, magazines, and journals, you will need to consult databases (on computers) and indexes (in bound volumes). *The Reader's Guide* and *The Magazine Index Plus* list all subjects covered in popular magazines. *The New York Times Index* and *The National Newspaper Index* list subjects covered in newspapers each year. In addition, nearly every subject field has its own specialized indexes and databases; ask the librarian for help.

Make a list of the periodicals and pages you want, including the date. You may need to check the *holdings file,* the list of periodicals your library carries. Sometimes you can read articles right on the computer screen. Otherwise the article will be available in a bound volume, in a loose copy, or on microfilm.

■ OTHER LIBRARY RESOURCES

Media Section

Slides, filmstrips, videotapes, recordings, computer programs, and so forth are housed in the media section and indexed in the library catalog.

The Pamphlet File

Sometimes called the *vertical file* or *clip file*, the *pamphlet file* stores clippings and pamphlets. It is an especially good source of material pertaining to local areas such as your state or home town. You'll need to ask a librarian for access.

Interlibrary Loan

At your request and with enough time, your library can obtain copies of books and photocopies of articles from other libraries.

Access to the Library from Home

Increasingly, college and public libraries allow their subscribers access to databases from their home computers. You may need to install special software or enter your password for this service.

See "A List of Valuable Sources" at the back of this book.

Getting Information Online

For most subjects, the Internet and electronic databases are increasingly the first places to look for information. As in the college library, to make full use of the Internet you will need to master the use of search terms. For a review, see the chapter "Three Essential Research Skills."

■ Use Several Avenues of Information

Most people rely on the "default" search engine provided by their Internet server as their usual avenue onto the Web. However, any one search engine will find at most only a small fraction of the websites actually available on a particular subject. For thorough research you should explore a variety of ways to find information.

Search engines such as *AltaVista* and *Yahoo* allow you to search through lists of subtopics or to type in a combination of search terms. These will lead you to websites. Be sure to use several different search engines. Two excellent ones to try are <www.google.com> and <www.northernlight.com>.

Metasearchers simultaneously search a number of search engines. Try <www.SavvySearch.com>, <www.Highway61.com>, and <www.Dogpile.com>.

Reference pages are assembled by researchers in a specific field, providing links to information not necessarily covered by search engines. Some are listed on the homepages of search engines; others can be found through Virtual Library at <www.vlib.org/Overview.html>, the homepages of libraries, or the faculty pages at colleges and universities.

Full-text databases allow you to read online all or part of the articles they list. Look on your library's homepage for *FirstSearch* and *Lexis-Nexis*.

Research libraries such as the Library of Congress and the New York Public Library have websites that you can consult—giving you the opportunity to look at major listings of books and in some cases databases as well. Use a search engine to find a specific library, or check the comprehensive list at <www.library.usask.ca/hywebcat>.

Homepages of colleges and universities can link you to libraries and course materials developed by college faculty: reading lists, syllabuses, and so forth. You can find these homepages through search engines. Try using the name of a particular college or your topic phrase plus "college."

Government agencies and nonprofit organizations provide valuable statistics and other information through their websites. Use a search engine and add "government" to your search terms. Look for websites with *.gov* or *.org* in their addresses.

News and entertainment organizations provide detailed information through their websites about a wide variety of topics. Some organizations, such as the *New York Times* and the *Christian Science Monitor,* allow search and retrieval from their archives.

See "A List of Valuable Sources" at the back of this book.

SIZING UP A WEBSITE

Although there are many legitimate websites from government agencies and well-known sources, the quality and accuracy of statements on the Internet vary widely. No one checks or credits the information in chat rooms and most bulletin boards.

How a website looks—the quality of its graphics—doesn't necessarily indicate the quality of its information. Here are some signs to look for:

Signs of a Questionable Website

- No author or organization listed on the page
- No date of last revision

- Typographical and grammar errors

- Bias or one-sided information. Commercial sites (.com) have something to sell; organizations favoring one side of a controversy may not present the other side fairly. Be skeptical and look for a variety of sources and views.

Signs of a Reliable Website

- A well-known author and sponsoring organization

- Regular updating of the site

- Presentation of the topic in depth—rather than a site for children, for instance

- Links to good websites (and links to this one from good sites)

- Documentation of the sources of information used by the author

■ CAUTIONS FOR RESEARCH ON THE INTERNET

The Internet can take up all of your research time. If you're not careful, you can get lost—adding too many subtopics or switching to new topics until your project loses its shape and you've run out of time. Researching electronically can become a mesmerizing activity, and you might find that at the end of a pleasant afternoon there is nothing to report. Allow a limited time—thirty to sixty minutes—just to follow the links from different websites that interest you.

The Internet is not a substitute for reading. Be sure you balance your Internet articles with books and periodicals. Many subjects are absent or treated superficially on the Internet.

Websites are not like video games. They don't necessarily progress to higher and higher levels. A good source might lead you to a superficial or irrelevant source.

Remember to bookmark. You may never be able to return to some sources you come across. Be methodical about using "bookmarks" (often called "favorites") when using your own computer. When you're using another computer, write down each Internet address with the title of the article.

For more detailed help with online research, see *Rules of Thumb for Online Research,* by Diana Roberts Wienbroer.

Writing the Research Paper

You've collected all sorts of information. You have a folder, maybe even a box, full of notes. Now you have to decide what to share with the reader. Are you going to just hand the reader the box? You need to decide what's most important to share with your reader.

■ Write a First Draft

If you try to write your final paper in one draft, you put yourself under too much pressure to make everything perfect the first time around.

Discover Your Own Perspective

After you have read and understood your sources, put your notes, books, and magazines aside in order to find your own position on your topic. Spend time freewriting or listing ideas until you know what you think about the topic. You might go back to the sentence you wrote before you began your research—the controlling idea. Is this still your main point? If not, write a new one.

Organize Your Thoughts and Write a Quick First Draft

The trick to a good first draft is to write it without consulting your notes. That way your paper will be in your own style, and you will write only what is clear to you. Later you can consult your notes for facts and quotations to add to your initial draft.

Without consulting your notes, develop a short informal outline. Put all the major points you plan to make into a logical arrangement. Avoid merely giving a part of your paper to each source you read; instead, give a part to each of the points you want to make.

Write a draft of your entire paper. Do this also without consulting your notes or your sources, just from memory. Be sure to include a paragraph for each topic in your informal outline. Explain information as you understand it; don't check the details yet.

Write to persuade. Remember that you are the authority. Use the facts that you remember to back up your position. Anticipate the reader's questions and doubts, and respond to them ahead of time.

Don't try for fancy words and long sentences. Tell what you know, emphasizing in your own words what is most important.

Four concerns you can defer until later:

- The perfect introduction: Once you see how your paper comes out, you can go back and improve your introduction.

- Spelling and punctuation: Save this concern until the revision stage.

- Documentation: You will add this information to your second draft.

- Length: You don't have to aim for a certain length yet. When you have a full first draft, you'll begin to see where information and explanations are needed.

■ INCORPORATE INFORMATION: QUOTATIONS, PARAPHRASE, SUMMARY, AND VISUALS

Once you have a first draft, you need to consult your notes. Read them and see which notes relate to the main points of your first draft. Select from your notes only the support you need for your own points. Disregard material that does not pertain to your main points—it will only distract your reader.

General Guidelines for Incorporating Information

- Don't download or copy hunks of information. Set your sources aside and write information in your own words.

- As you insert a fact, quotation, or opinion from a source, note the author and the exact page where you found it. For APA documentation style, also note the copyright date.

- Don't overload your paragraphs with facts and quotations.

- Weave together several sources rather than using one source at a time.

- Lead into facts or quotations gracefully. Often it's most effective to use the name of the author in your sentence.

  > According to D. M. Larsen, . . .

  > Regina Schrambling, in "Tex-Mex Pizza," tells how . . .

- When you present a fact or quotation, relate it to the larger point you are making. In your own words, clarify the importance of the fact or quotation.

Balance the different ways of presenting information: *direct quotation, paraphrase,* and *summary.* In addition, computers now make it easy to include photographs, charts, and other helpful visuals.

Direct Quotation

In direct quotation, you use the *exact* wording from your material and surround the words with quotation marks. Even if you use only a phrase or a key word, you must indicate that it has been taken from another source by placing it within quotation marks. The chapter "Quotation Marks" (pages 40–43) will help you with the correct form for quotations.

Keep quotations secondary to your own ideas. Each quotation should illustrate a definite point you want to make. Before and after the quotation, stress your point. Maintain your own writing style throughout the paper.

Direct quotation is often overused in research papers. Don't use many quotations, and keep the ones you do use brief—two or three lines at most. When you can, work a *phrase* from the author into your own sentence. Your paper should not be more than 15 percent quotation.

- *Do quote:*

  Memorable and distinctive phrases
  Strong statements of opinion by authorities

- *Do not quote:*

  Facts and statistics (He was born in 1945.)
  Standard terminology in a field (asthma, velocity)

To avoid relying too heavily on quotation, make a point of using the other two methods of paraphrase and summary.

Paraphrase

When you paraphrase, you take someone else's idea or information and put it into your own words. Usually you paraphrase one statement, not more than a few lines, at one time. A good place for paraphrase, rather than quotation, is in telling basic facts: dates, statistics, places, and so forth. The pitfall in paraphrasing comes when you stick too closely to your source's phrasing, writing things you don't fully understand in language not really your own. Instead, read the passage (making sure you understand it), close the book, and write your paraphrase in plain English.

You can't half paraphrase. That is, if you mix in some of the author's exact words, you must use quotation marks around them.

Summary

When you summarize, you take a substantial amount of material and condense it. You can summarize a long passage, several pages, a chapter, or even an entire article or book. Use summary when you want to acknowledge a conflicting idea or when you want to cover a related idea without too much detail.

Visuals

Visuals—charts, maps, drawings, photographs—can communicate a large amount of information in a small space.

- **Don't just stick in a visual for effect.** First be certain that the illustration gives additional information or clarifies a statement in your paper. It has to have a purpose.

- **Be sure that your illustration is clear.** Enlarge it if you need to.

- **Give each visual a caption** and place it into the text right at the point where you have discussed it; however, if the visuals will be too disruptive to the paper, add them in an appendix at the end.

- **Give the source of the illustration if you did not create it.** (For proper documentation, see page 119.)

■ PREPARE YOUR FINAL PAPER

Revise Your Essay

Copying over a first draft is not revising. Work on the following aspects of your paper:

- Make sure that you have written clearly, not in an artificial style.

- Be sure that each paragraph has one clear point and is logically connected to the paragraphs before and after it. Omit or move information that doesn't fit with a paragraph's main point.

- Look for places where the reader will need more information in order to follow your point.

- Check for smoothness leading into and out of direct quotations, paraphrases, and summaries.

Edit Your Essay

Patiently examine the following aspects of your paper:

- Accuracy of quotations, numbers, and the spelling of names

- Accuracy and format of documentation

- Manuscript format (See the chapter "Format of College Papers," pages 82–84.)

Proofread your paper both on the screen and on the final printed copy.

WRITING ABOUT LITERATURE

When you are asked to write about literature, make sure of your teacher's expectations. Some teachers want a *summary* of your reading, in which you tell the main points of what you've read, followed by your evaluation. However, most literature teachers want you to stress an important idea about the reading and to demonstrate the details that gave you your idea. Usually, you will rely on details from the text itself, but you may also be asked to write a research paper about literature, incorporating information and ideas from scholars in the field.

■ GENERAL GUIDELINES FOR LITERATURE PAPERS

You can adapt the methods described here for writing about other arts such as film, music, painting, dance, and architecture.

Gather Your First Impressions of the Topic

Your first reading should be a time to enjoy the text, to respond without the pressure to come up with answers. A good idea is to keep a reading journal in which you jot down your reactions to the text as they come to you.

After you finish reading the work of literature, write down your first impressions, checking the assigned topic. Write quickly, without pausing, to get your ideas on paper. This freewriting will help you to discover the main idea you want to stress.

Reread the Text

Search for evidence to support your main idea and also for evidence that might lead you to modify it. The evidence could include specific quotations, details, events, or subtleties of style. Make notes as you reread, and mark passages you may wish to quote.

Organize Your Essay

Do not merely follow the order of what you read. Instead, decide on your main idea, the points you want to stress, and the best sequence to make them clear.

Omit Plot Summary and the Author's Life

Unless you've been asked to, do not include a detailed plot summary repeating all the events of the story. Remember, the teacher already knows what the book says but does not know your ideas about the assignment. Your job is to show the reader your point about the story rather than to tell the story. However, you will refer to details from the plot when you give examples to support your ideas.

Do not include a summary of the author's life in your essay unless you have been asked to do so.

Use Evidence to Back Up Your Points

For each main point, explain which details from the reading gave you that idea. In some cases, *briefly* quote the author. After referring to a detail or quoting a passage, always explain why that detail or passage supports your point.

Incorporate Quotations Gracefully

Keep quotations few and, in most cases, brief. Include only quotations that help to show the point you are making. First, make your point. Then lead into the quotation by briefly referring to its context. Make clear whether you are quoting the author or a character. When you quote a character, refer to the character by name rather than to the author.

After the quotation, particularly if it is a sentence or more, comment on its significance—tie it to the point of your paragraph.

For specific skills of quotation, including how to quote poetry, see the chapter "Quotation Marks," pages 40–43.

■ RESEARCH PAPERS ABOUT LITERATURE

One of the major differences between a literary research paper and other documented papers is that in a literary paper your main focus is on the text itself. The research takes second place to your own close reading of the piece you are writing about. In writing a research paper about literature, follow the guidelines for all literature papers, with these additional considerations.

Be Clear about the Assignment

Make sure you understand what you are being asked to do: Are you being asked to compare your ideas to those of critics? Are you being asked to find out about the historical context surrounding a piece of work? The specific assignment will dictate the kind of sources you should choose.

Freewrite Before Doing Research

Before reading any critics, freewrite about the topic, if your teacher has given you one; otherwise write about your thoughts and feelings in response to the reading. Write out several ideas that you might emphasize in an essay.

Choose Several Critics to Read

Not all critical studies are equal. To find the best critics to read, a good place to start is with the introduction and any list of recommended readings in the edition of the work you are studying. You can also look at recommended sources in anthologies (such as *The Norton Anthology of English Literature*). The most complete listings of books and articles about literature are in the *MLA* (Modern Language Association) *Bibliography*. Also, your professor may guide you to the best critical studies.

Read the critics carefully and critically. Look for ideas that correspond to your own experience of the work. Be open to reconsidering and refining your first impressions, even changing them completely at times. But remember that your experience as a reader has value and must be the heart of your essay.

Incorporate Ideas of Critics into Your Essay

For most assignments, the critics you've read should not dominate your essay. Organize your paper around your ideas, presenting one idea at a time, rather than presenting one critic at a time. Don't get bogged down in the ideas of critics. Remember that your ideas are still the center of your paper.

In most cases paraphrase or summarize the ideas of critics, quoting them directly only when their phrasing is significant or memorable—when you will comment on the critic's wording. Always relate a critic's ideas to the main thrust or thesis of your essay.

Remember that your primary subject is the literature itself. It offers the best evidence for your ideas. The majority of your examples and quotations will come from the literary text.

■ CONVENTIONS OF LITERARY ESSAYS

Titles

- <u>Underline</u> or *italicize* titles of books, periodicals, plays, films, and television programs. Put "quotation marks" around titles of stories, poems, essays, and one-act plays.

- Capitalize the first word, major words, and words of six letters or more.

- The title of your paper should express your main idea, not just give the title of the text.

> The Uses of Rhyme in Robert Browning's "My Last Duchess"

For detailed instructions about titles, see the chapter "Titles: Underlines, Italics, or Quotation Marks," page 44.

Identifying the Author and Title

- Use the author's full name the first time you mention it. Thereafter, use the full name or last name, not the first name by itself.

- Be sure to identify the title and author early in your essay, even if you've already done so in your title.

> In "A Fly Buzzed When I Died," Emily Dickinson presents a disturbing vision of the moment of death.

> In <u>King Lear</u>, Shakespeare examines a king's assumptions about language.

> "A Rose for Emily," by William Faulkner, is a study of changing social classes.

> Laura Esquivel's <u>Like Water for Chocolate</u> explores the consequences of passion.

You can use this type of sentence to begin your essay, or you can introduce the general topic (death, language, social classes, passion) and then identify the specific text you will examine.

Note carefully the punctuation in these examples. Remember that a comma or period goes inside quotation marks.

Verb Tenses

In writing your paper, use the present tense, the most graceful tense for referring to a poem or story.

> Early in the novel, Elizabeth misjudges Darcy.

> Yeats portrays a "glimmering girl" who can never be captured.

■ BIBLIOGRAPHICAL INFORMATION

Page References

In your paper, indicate the location of each quotation from your primary source by putting the page number in parentheses following the quotation.

> The first chapter of Hawthorne's <u>The Scarlet Letter</u> puns on the mix of church and state in the "steeple-crowned hats" of the Puritans (35).

If the quotation is indented, put the period before the parenthesis; otherwise, put the period last.

- For a poem (such as Coleridge's "The Rime of the Ancient Mariner"), give the line numbers.

  > Water, water, every where,
  > And all the boards did shrink; Water, water, every where,
  > Nor any drop to drink. (119–122)

- For the Bible, give the abbreviated title of the specific book, with chapter and verse.

  > To every thing there is a season, and a time to every purpose under the heaven. (Eccles. 3.1)

- For a play (such as Shakespeare's *Antony and Cleopatra*), give act, scene, and lines.

    Age cannot wither her, nor custom stale
    Her infinite variety. (2.2.234–235)

- When quoting from or referring to an idea from a critic, mention the critic's name, and give the source when appropriate.

    Eudora Welty, in the foreword of <u>To the Lighthouse</u>, says that, in this novel, Virginia Woolf "has shown us the shape of the human spirit" (xii).

Works Cited

Your *Works Cited* should include an entry for every source you cited within the paper, including the edition of the literary text that you have used.

```
Hughes, Langston. "Mother to Son."
        Selected Poems of Langston Hughes.
    New York: Knopf, 1970. 187.
```

If the book was originally published in an edition different from yours, put the original date of publication after the title:

```
Woolf, Virginia. To the Lighthouse. 1927.
    San Diego: Harcourt, 1981.
```

If you used a poem or short story in an anthology or an introduction or a preface from a book, you need to include a citation for the author and specific short work you referred to, as well as all the information for the book, including the pages covered.

```
Meltzer, Richard. "The Aesthetics of
        Rock." Penguin Book of Rock & Roll
        Writing. Ed. Clinton Heylin. New
        York: Viking, 1992. 81-87.

Welty, Eudora. Foreword. To the
        Lighthouse. By Virginia Woolf. San
        Diego: Harcourt, 1981. vii-xii.
```

For further details, see the chapter "Documentation: The MLA Style," pages 115–129.

PLAGIARISM (CHEATING)

Penalties for plagiarism can be severe: failure of the course or expulsion from the college. Unintentional plagiarism is still plagiarism, so be careful and know the rules.

Plagiarism means *writing facts, quotations, or opinions that you got from someone else without identifying your source; or using someone else's words without putting quotation marks around them.*

To Avoid Plagiarism

- Always give credit for a fact, quotation, or opinion whether you read it, retrieved it electronically, saw it on television, heard it on the radio, or learned it from another person— even when you use your own wording.

- When you use another person's wording—even a phrase— always put quotation marks around the person's exact words.

- Write your first draft with your books closed. Do not write with a book or magazine open next to you. Don't go back and forth taking ideas from a source and writing your paper.

- Don't let your sources take over the essay. Tell what you know well in your own style, stressing what you find most important.

DOCUMENTATION: THE MLA STYLE

The word *documentation* means that you have added two elements to your paper:

Citations of sources
List of works cited

■ CITATIONS

When you give citations in a paper, you tell specifically where you got a piece of information—in other words, the *source* you used.

WHEN TO GIVE YOUR SOURCE

You must acknowledge in your paper the source of

- A direct quotation

- A statistic

- An idea

- Someone else's opinion

- Concrete facts

- Information taken from the computer

- Illustrations, photographs, or charts—if not your own

- Information not commonly known

Even if you *paraphrase* (put someone else's words into your own words) or *summarize* (condense someone else's words or ideas), you still must acknowledge the source of your information.

If a fact is common knowledge (George Washington was the first president), you don't have to give your source.

HOW TO USE PARENTHETICAL CITATION

The MLA (Modern Language Association) style of documentation is used for courses in English and in foreign languages. MLA style uses *parenthetical citation*. In this system you give your source in parentheses immediately after you give the information. Your reader can then find the complete listing of each source at the end of the paper in your Works Cited section.

The four most common citations are

• Author and page number

• Title and page number

• Page number only

• Secondhand quotations

For any citation it is crucial that the first word of the citation match the first word of the corresponding entry on your Works Cited page in the back of your paper.

Author and Page Number

Put the author's last name and the page number in parentheses immediately after the information:

> (Schrambling 125).

Notice that there is no "p." and no comma. In the text it looks like this:

> Tex-Mex flavored pizza has become very popular (Schrambling 125).

If your citation comes at the end of a sentence, the period goes outside the last parenthesis. (Exception: With indented quotations, the period goes before the parenthesis.)

Where a page number is not available, give the number of a section (sec.), paragraph (para.), or line (l.) if possible.

Title and Page Number

Often articles, editorials, pamphlets, and other materials have no author listed. In such cases, give only the first distinctive word of the title followed by the page number:

> The actual fat content of a frozen pizza may be more than the package claims ("A Meal" 19).

Note that you give the title of the specific article that you read, not the title of the newspaper, magazine, or reference book ("A Meal" not <u>Consumer Reports</u>).

Page Number Only

Put only the page number in parentheses when you have already mentioned the author's name.

> Jim Cohen makes low-fat pizzas "from start to finish on the grill" (93).

When possible, use this method of citation. Mentioning the author's name as you present information makes your paper more cohesive and readable.

Secondhand Quotations

When you quote someone who has been quoted in one of your sources, use *qtd. in* (quoted in):

> Evelyne Slomon, author of numerous cookbooks, refers to the years between 1920 and the early 50s as the "golden age of pizza in America" (qtd. in O'Neill 59).

In this example Slomon said it, although you found it in O'Neill. Note that Slomon will not be listed in your Works Cited; O'Neill will be.

Special Cases

Electronic Sources

- Articles and books originally in print

  For sources originally in print but read on the screen or printed from the computer, follow the same format as you would for the printed versions, but without page numbers. In your Works Cited you will indicate where you found the source—either CD-ROM or the Internet address.

  > Another way to reduce fat in deep-dish pizza is by substituting turkey sausage and part-skim mozzarella (Gooch).

- Other electronic sources—including websites, online postings, videos, and television or radio programs

Most electronic sources do not have page numbers. You may give the name in parentheses, but you can be more precise by indicating the format and incorporating the speaker or organization smoothly into your sentence.

> In a discussion of how to reduce the fat content of traditional pizza recipes, Jim Powers posted a suggestion: substitute a fat-free flour tortilla for the pizza crust.

> Professor Carlo Mangone, who teaches nutrition at the Second University of Naples, said in a radio interview that there are only two classic pizzas—the marinara and the margherita.

Interview or Speech

If your source is an interview, lecture, or speech, include the person's name in your paragraph and use no parenthetical citation.

> Kevin O'Reilly, owner of K. O'Reilly's Pizza, reports that pepperoni pizza outsells the low-fat versions ten to one.

Two Sources by the Same Author

When you have two or more sources by the same author, use the first identifying words to indicate the title of the work you're citing.

> Julia Child advises that the dough be chilled to slow the rising (In Julia's 6).

> or

> Some chefs chill the dough to slow the rising (Child, In Julia's 6).

Organization as Author

Sometimes the author is an organization.

> According to the United States Department of Agriculture, one slice of cheese pizza has 255 calories (1).

> or

> One slice of cheese pizza has 255 calories (United States Dept. of Agriculture 1).

Note: Do not abbreviate in your sentence—only in the parenthetical citation.

Illustration or Graphics

- If the artist's name is given and the visual (such as an editorial cartoon) is not an illustration of the text surrounding it, put the last name and page number in parentheses below the graphic.

     (Chaney 69).

- If the artist's name is given but the visual illustrates the text with which it appears, give the artist's name and then the author's name and the page.

     (Acevedo in Cohen 97).

     Note that only Cohen will be listed in your Works Cited.

- If the artist is not identified (for instance, in an advertisement) give the author (or owner of the copyright) and page where the illustration appeared.

     (Kraft Foods 5).

HOW OFTEN TO GIVE CITATIONS

When several facts in a row within one paragraph all come from the same page of a source, use one citation to cover them all. Place the citation after the last fact, but alert the reader at the outset with a phrase such as "According to Janet Tynan, . . ."

Do not, however, wait more than a few lines to let the reader know where the facts came from. The citation must be in the same paragraph as the facts.

Remember: You must give citations for information, not just for quotations.

SAMPLE PARAGRAPH USING CITATIONS

On the following page is a sample paragraph in which you can see how various citations are used. (You will rarely have this many citations in one short paragraph.) The sources cited here can be found among the works cited on page 129.

MLA

When the first pizzeria opened in New York City in 1905, it introduced the classic Italian pizza--bread dough covered with tomato sauce and cheese ("Pizza" 490). Now, almost a century later, the simple pizza has been transformed into an American creation that reflects this country's love of diversity. In addition to the classic version, pizza lovers can now savor just about every combination and concoction imaginable. The National Association of Pizza Operators reports that "Pizza makers have tried virtually every type of food on pizzas, including peanut butter and jelly, bacon and eggs, and mashed potatoes" (qtd. in "A Meal" 21). Gourmet versions, such as the Tex-Mex, which Regina Schrambling says is "welcomed by most Americans," continue to satisfy our taste for the unusual (125). From France comes the pissaladière, which adds fresh herbs, black olives, and anchovies (Child, Bertholle, and Beck 151). Even America's exports reflect our adaptability; for example, Domino's uses pickled ginger and chicken on its pizzas in India (Crossette 2). You might have to travel to Italy to get real Italian pizza; but you can eat your way across this country-- and the world--sampling several hundred modern versions of pizza made the American way.

■ Works Cited

When you were gathering your material, you may have used a "working *bibliography*," a list of potential sources. However, now that you have written your paper and have seen which sources you actually did use, you must include a separate page at the end of the paper listing your Works Cited.

There are four major points to understand about a Works Cited page:

- List *only* those sources that you actually referred to in your paper.

- List the whole article, or essay, or book—not just the pages you used.

- *Alphabetize* your list of sources by the authors' last names. If no author is listed, alphabetize by the first main word in the title.

- Format is extremely important to many teachers. Pay special attention to order, spacing, and punctuation.

  - ~ Put the author's last name first.

  - ~ Double-space the entire list.

  - ~ Start each entry at the left margin.

  - ~ Indent the second and third lines of each entry five spaces.

  - ~ Notice that most of the items in a citation are separated by periods.

  - ~ Leave one space after a comma, colon, or period.

  - ~ Put a period at the end of each entry.

Examples of the format for specific entries follow. A sample Works Cited appears on page 129.

SPECIFIC ENTRIES

Book

Author. <u>Title</u>. City: Publisher, date.

> Love, Louise. <u>The Complete Book of Pizza</u>.
> Evanston, IL: Sassafras, 1980.

Note: If the city of publication is not well known, give the two-letter Post Office abbreviation for the state, without periods.

Article in a Magazine

Author. "Title of Article." <u>Title of Periodical</u> Date: page(s).

> Schrambling, Regina. "Tex-Mex Pizza."
> <u>Working Woman</u> Feb. 1988: 125.

Article in a Newspaper

Author (if given). "Title of Article." <u>Title of Newspaper</u> Complete date, section number or title: page(s).

> Crossette, Barbara. "Burgers Are the
> Globe's Fast Food? Not So Fast." <u>New
> York Times</u> 26 Nov. 2000, sec. 4:2.

If the section is designated by a letter instead of a number or a name, put the colon after the date and then give the section letter before the page number.

> 26 Nov. 2000: A12.

Article or Story in a Collection or Anthology

Author of article. "Title of Article." <u>Title of Book</u>. Editor of book. City: Publisher, date. Pages covered by article.

> Cook, Joan Marble. "Italy: Myths and
> Truths." <u>Italy</u>. Ed. Ronald Steel.
> New York: Wilson, 1963, 31–37.

Article in a Scholarly Journal

Author. "Title of Article." <u>Title of Journal</u> Volume number (Complete date): pages covered by article.

> Larsen, D. M., et al. "The Effects of Flour Type and Dough Retardation Time on Sensory Characteristics of Pizza Crust." <u>Cereal Chemistry</u> 70 (Nov.-Dec. 1993): 647-50.

Material from Computers

Note: If complete information about your source is not available—for example, the name of the author—just list whatever information you have, in the order given below, without blank spaces.

Standalone Database or CD-ROM

Author. "Title." (or the heading of the material you read) <u>Title of the entire work</u> and publishing information of original in print, if known. <u>Title of the database</u>. Publication medium. Vendor (if relevant). Electronic publication date.

> Gooch, Annette. "Deep-Dish Dough: Leaner Chicago-Style Pizza from Scratch." <u>Newsday</u> 16 Mar. 1997 sec. Food Day: 1. <u>Newsbank Newsday</u>. CD-ROM. 1999.

Online Source or Website

Author or organization. "Title of section, if given." <u>Title of the complete work</u>. Date of publication or last revision. Sponsoring organization if different from author. Date you viewed it <address of the Website>.

> United States. Dept. of Agriculture. "Calories and Weight: The USDA Pocket Guide." <u>DietSearch: News and Articles</u>. Mar. 1990. Diet Search. 10 Jan. 2001 <http:www.dietsearch.com/article/ calories/htm>.

Direct E-Mail to You (not a discussion group)

Author of e-mail (title or area of expertise, professional affiliation). "Subject line." E-mail to the author (meaning you) date.

```
Brooks, Evelyn [Marketing researcher,
     Moorpark, CA, Food Association].
     "Re: Pizza." E-mail to the author.
     7 Jan 2001.
```

Posting to a Discussion Group

Real name of author. "The subject line of the article." Online posting. The date of the posting. The group to which it was sent—if there are multiple groups separate them by a comma. Date you viewed it <where the article can be retrieved>.

```
Claudia. "Re: I Love Pizza." Online
     posting. 3 Jan. 2000.
     alt.support.diet. 10 Jan. 2001
     <http://www.deja.com>.
```

Encyclopedia

"Title of Article." <u>Title of Encyclopedia</u>. Year of the edition.

```
"Pizza." Encyclopaedia Britannica:
     Micropaedia. 1997 ed.
```

Special Cases

No Author Listed

Alphabetize according to the first main word of the title. Include *A, An, The,* but do not use them when alphabetizing. For example, this article will be alphabetized with *M* in the Works Cited:

```
"A Meal That's Easy as Pie: How to Pick a
     Pizza That's Good and Healthful."
     Consumer Reports Jan. 1997: 19-23.
```

Two or More Authors

Give the last name first for the first author only; use first name first for the other author(s).

> Child, Julia, Louisette Bertholle, and
>   Simone Beck. <u>Mastering the Art of
>   French Cooking</u>. Vol. 1. New York:
>   Knopf, 1966.

Additional Works by the Same Author

Use three hyphens and a period in place of the author's name and alphabetize the works by title.

> Child, Julia. <u>In Julia's Kitchen with
>   Master Chefs</u>. New York: Knopf, 1995.
> ---. <u>Julia's Kitchen Wisdom: Essential
>   Techniques and Recipes from a
>   Lifetime of Cooking.</u> New York:
>   Knopf, 2000.

Pamphlet

Follow the format for a book. Often an organization is the publisher. If no author is listed, begin with the title. If no date is listed, use n.d. for no date.

> United States. Dept. of Agriculture.
>   <u>Eating Better When Eating Out: Using
>   the Dietary Guidelines</u>. Washington:
>   GPO, n.d.

Radio or Television Program

Give the name of the speaker. Underline the title of the program. Give the network, if any, then the station call letters and city. Then list the date of the broadcast.

> Mangone, Carlo. <u>Weekend Edition Saturday</u>.
>   Natl. Public Radio. WNYC, New York.
>   31 May 1997.

Videocassette or Audio Recording

List the author, director, or performer; the title; the format; the distributor; and the release date.

> Smith, Jeff. <u>Frugal Gourmet: Sauces and
>   Seasonings--Garlic! Garlic!</u>
>   Videocassette. Mpi Home Video, 1992.

Interview, Speech, or Lecture

Give the person's name and position, the kind of presentation (personal or telephone interview, speech, or classroom lecture), the location, and the date.

> O'Reilly, Kevin [Owner, K O'Reilly's
>   Pizza]. Personal interview. Troy,
>   MO. 2 Jan. 2001.

Illustration or Graphics

- If the artist's name is given and the visual (such as an editorial cartoon) is not an illustration of the text surrounding it, give the artist's name, the type of visual it is (cartoon, photograph, chart), and the complete information for the source in which it appears, including the date viewed or the page.

> Chaney, Tom. Cartoon. <u>New Yorker</u> 30 Jan.
>   1989: 69.

- If the artist's name is given but the visual illustrates the text with which it appears, give only the author and other information for the text.

> Cohen, Jim. "Simple, Healthful Grilling."
>   <u>Food & Wine</u> June 1997: 92-98+.

MLA

- If the artist is not identified (for instance, in an
  advertisement) give the author (or owner of the copyright)
  and complete information on the source, including the page
  where the illustration appeared.

> Kraft Foods. Advertisement. <u>Eating Well</u>
>   July/Aug. 1997: 5.
>
> Cedarlane Natural Foods. Chart. <u>Low Fat</u>
>   <u>Vegetarian Pizza Veggie Wrap</u>. 31
>   July 1997. 7 Jan. 2001 <http://www.
>   cedarlane foods.com/p00ag.htm>.

A sample of a Works Cited page follows. It illustrates a variety
of sources and therefore is longer than you probably will need.
The left-hand page identifies the category of each source.

MLA

Explanations of Works Cited

Book, single author ⟶

Repeated author (same author as above) ⟶

Book, three authors, one volume cited, (repeated author with first citing of co-authors) ⟶

Article or chapter in an edited collection [Use this form also for a single selection from an anthology.] ⟶

Newspaper article ⟶

Article in a scholarly journal, more than three authors ⟶

Radio program [Use this form also for a television program.] ⟶

Magazine article (monthly), unsigned ⟶

Interview [Use this form also for a lecture or speech.] ⟶

Encyclopedia article, unsigned ⟶
Magazine article, signed ⟶

Article on the Internet, organization as author ⟶

Works Cited

Child, Julia. In Julia's Kitchen with Master Chefs.
New York: Knopf, 1995.

---. Julia's Kitchen Wisdom: Essential Techniques and
Recipes from a Lifetime of Cooking. New York:
Knopf, 2000.

Child, Julia, Louisette Bertholle, and Simone Beck.
Mastering the Art of French Cooking. Vol. 1. New
York: Knopf, 1966.

Cook, Joan Marble. "Italy: Myths and Truths." Italy.
Ed. Ronald Steel. New York: Wilson, 1963, 31-37.

Crossette, Barbara. "Burgers Are the Globe's Fast
Food? Not So Fast." New York Times
26 Nov. 2000, sec. 4: 2.

Larsen, D. M., et al. "The Effects of Flour Type and
Dough Retardation Time on Sensory Characteristics
of Pizza Crust." Cereal Chemistry 70 (1993):
647-50.

Mangone, Carlo. Weekend Edition Saturday. National
Public Radio. WNYC, New York. 31 May 1997.

"A Meal That's Easy as Pie: How to Pick a Pizza That's
Good and Healthful." Consumer Reports Jan. 1997:
19-23.

O'Reilly, Kevin [Owner, K O'Reilly's Pizza]. Personal
interview. Troy, MO. 2 Jan. 2001.

"Pizza." Encyclopaedia Britannica: Micropaedia. 1997 ed.

Schrambling, Regina. "Tex-Mex Pizza." Working Woman
Feb. 1988: 125.

United States. Dept. of Agriculture. "Calories and
Weight: The USDA Pocket Guide." DietSearch: News
and Articles. March 1990. Diet Search. 10 Jan. 2001
<http:www.dietsearch.com/article/calories/htm>.

DOCUMENTATION: THE APA STYLE

The APA (American Psychological Association) style is used for courses in the social sciences, such as psychology, sociology, anthropology, and economics, and for some of the life sciences (consult your professor).

This style places the last name of the author and the date of publication in parentheses immediately after any research information. At the end of the paper, a complete list of sources (References) provides the details about the particular books, articles, and other documents you used.

■ PARENTHETICAL CITATIONS

For the basics of using parenthetical citations, see pages 115 and 119.

Here are the most common forms for APA style:

For Books and Articles:
Author and Date of Publication

The preferred form is to use the author's last name in your sentence, followed by the date of publication in parentheses:

```
Schrambling (1988, February) described
the popularity of Tex-Mex flavored pizza.
```

Note that in APA style, the author's work is referred to in the past tense ("described").

When the author is not mentioned in your sentence, the parentheses will contain both the author's last name and the date of publication.

```
Tex-Mex pizza became very popular in the
1980s (Schrambling, 1988, February).
```

If no author is listed, give only the first distinctive word of the title, followed by the date of publication. Give the title of the specific article that you read, not the title of the newspaper, magazine, or reference book.

Page Number for Direct Quotations

For a direct quotation, give the page number, with the abbreviation p. or pp. after the date.

> Cohen (1997, June, p. 93) made low-fat
> pizzas "from start to finish on the
> grill."

APA does not require the page number for a paraphrase but recommends it if the source is more than a few pages long.

Special Cases

Websites

When you have used an entire website as a general reference, refer to the website in your sentence and give its address in parentheses:

> Domino's Pizza posted nutritional
> information on its website
> (http:hotpizza2u.com).

Articles and Books Originally in Print but Retrieved Electronically

If the article or book appeared in print first, cite the author and original date of publication, even if you read the material online.

Personal Communications (e-mails, interviews, lectures)

When your source communicated with you personally, write, in parentheses, personal communication and the date (month day, year):

> O'Reilly, owner of K. O'Reilly's Pizza,
> reported that pepperoni pizza outsells
> the low-fat versions ten to one (personal
> communication, January 2, 2001).

More than One Author

For **two authors,** join the last names with *and* if you refer to them in your sentence or with an ampersand **(&)** if you cite them in parentheses. For **three to six authors,** give all the names for the first reference. Thereafter, use only the last name of the first author plus *et al.* (meaning "and others"). For **more than six authors,** give only the last name of the first author plus *et al.*

Two Sources by the Same Author

When you have two or more sources by one author, the different dates will indicate the different sources. When two sources by the same author have the same date, put a lowercase letter after the date to distinguish the source—Jones 1994a, Jones 1994b, and so on. Use the alphabetical order of the titles to assign letters.

SAMPLE PARAGRAPH USING CITATIONS

In the following paragraph, you can see how various citations are used. (You will rarely have this many citations in one short paragraph.) The sources cited here can be found among the references on page 138.

When the first pizzeria opened in New York City in 1905, it introduced the classic Italian pizza--bread dough covered with tomato sauce and cheese (Pizza 1997). Now, almost a century later, the simple pizza has been transformed into an American creation that reflects this country's love of diversity. In addition to the classic version, pizza lovers can now savor just about every combination and concoction imaginable. The National Association of Pizza Operators reported that "Pizza makers have tried virtually every type of food on pizzas, including peanut butter and jelly,

bacon and eggs, and mashed potatoes" (qtd. in A
meal 1997, January, p. 21). Gourmet versions,
such as the Tex-Mex, which Schrambling (1988,
February, p. 125) said is "welcomed by most
Americans," continue to satisfy our taste for
the unusual. From France comes the
pissaladière, which adds fresh herbs, black
olives, and anchovies (Child, Bertholle, & Beck
1966, p. 151). Even America's exports reflect
our adaptability; for example, Domino's uses
pickled ginger and chicken on its pizzas in
India (Crossette, 2000, November 26). You might
have to travel to Italy to get real Italian
pizza; but you can eat your way across this
country--and the world--sampling several
hundred modern versions of pizza made the
American way.

■ REFERENCES

At the end of your paper, on a separate page, you will list the sources that were mentioned in your paper or cited in parentheses. For the basic rules of Reference pages, see the section on "Works Cited" in the chapter on the MLA style of documentation, page 121. In addition, the following rules apply:

Heading

The list is titled References. It should be centered, capitalizing only the first letter, with no underline, boldface, or quotation marks.

Authors' Names

- Alphabetize the list by authors' last names. Give only the initials for the first and middle names of authors. Give all names in reverse order, even for multiple authors. List all authors up to six, and then use *et al.* (meaning *and others*).

- For authors who have written more than one work, repeat the name for each entry. List the works in chronological order. If the works have the same date, add a letter to the date—2000a, 2000b, and so on—putting the titles in alphabetical order.

- If no author is listed, begin your entry with the title (but alphabetize by the first main word of the title—not *The, A,* or *An*).

Date of Publication

The date of publication for each entry is placed within parentheses right after the author's name (or after the title if no author is listed). For articles and other sources that indicate month or month and day, include this information—year, month day—without abbreviations.

Titles

- Capitalize only the first word of most titles and subtitles, but capitalize all main words of titles of newspapers, magazines, and scholarly journals.

- Use italics for the titles of books, newspapers, magazines, CD-ROMs, and websites. Titles of shorter works that appear inside the larger ones, such as articles and chapters, are printed without underlines, italics, or quotation marks.

Publisher

Do not abbreviate publishers' names; do abbreviate *and* with &. Do not include "Co.," "Inc.," or "Publisher," but do include "University" and "Press."

Pages

Use p. or pp. to indicate the pages for articles in periodicals or chapters in books.

SPECIFIC ENTRIES

For formats not listed, adapt the form for the MLA style.

Book or Pamphlet

Author (Date). *Title.* City: Publisher.

> Love, L. (1980). *The complete book of pizza.* Evanston, IL: Sassafras.

Article in a Magazine or Newspaper

Author (complete date, year first). Title of article. *Title of Periodical,* section (for newspapers): page(s).

> Crossette, B. (2000, November 26). Burgers are the globe's fast food? Not so fast. *New York Times,* section 4:2.

Article in a Collection or Anthology

Author of article (date). Title of article. In Editor of book (Ed.), *Title of book* (pages covered by article). City: Publisher.

> Cook, J. M. (1963). Italy: Myths and truths. In R. Steele (Ed.), *Italy.* (pp. 31–37). New York: Wilson.

Article in a Scholarly Journal

Author (date). Title of article. *Title of Journal Volume number:* pages covered by article.

> Larsen, D. M., et al. (1993). The effects of flour type and dough retardation time on sensory characteristics of pizza crust. *Cereal Chemistry 70:* pp. 647-650.

Material from Computers

If complete information about your source is not available—for example, the name of the author—just list whatever information you have, in the order given below, without blank spaces.

Standalone Database or CD-ROM

Author or organization. (original publication date). Title. (or the heading of the material you read) Title and publishing information of original in print, if known. Retrieved from Title of the database (Publication medium, Vendor [if relevant], date).

> Gooch, A. (1997, March 16). Deep-dish dough: Leaner Chicago-style pizza from scratch. *Newsday* Section Food Day: 1. Retrieved from *Newsbank Newsday* (CD-ROM, 1999).

Print Source Retrieved Online

Author or organization. (date of publication or last revision). Title of the article (if appropriate). Title of the Complete Publication. Pages or publishing information. Retrieved date from address of the website

> Perry, J. (2000, June 26). Operator! Get me the Web . . . and a pizza. *US News and World Report.* Retrieved

> January 10, 2001 from http://www.
> usnews.com/usnews/issue/000626/nycu/
> voice.htm

The "retrieved" date is the date you viewed it. Notice that you do not place a period after the Internet address.

A Specific Document on a Website

Author or organization (if known). (Date of publication or last revision). Title of the article. *Title of the Complete Work.* Retrieved date from address of the website.

> U.S. Department of Agriculture. (1990,
> March). Calories and weight: The
> USDA pocket guide. *DietSearch: News
> and articles.* Retrieved January 10,
> 2001 from http:www.dietsearch.
> com/article/calories/htm

An Entire Website

In the APA style, give the address of the website in parentheses at the end of your sentence—see "Website," page 131. Do not give the web address in your reference list.

E-Mail, Interview, Speech, or Lecture

In the APA style, you do not list any personal communications in your references because no one else can review the source. Do indicate the source clearly in your paper—see "Personal Communications," page 131.

Encyclopedia

Author of article if given. (date). Title of article. In *Title of encyclopedia* (Volume number, pages covered by article). City: Publisher.

> Pizza. (1997). In *The new encyclopaedia
> Britannica* (Vol. 9, p. 490).
> Chicago: Encyclopaedia Britannica.

The following page includes the references for the sample paragraph on pages 132–33.

References

Child, J. (1995). *In Julia's kitchen with master chefs*. New York: Knopf.

Child, J. (2000). *Julia's kitchen wisdom: Essential techniques and recipes from a lifetime of cooking*. New York: Knopf.

Child, J., Bertholle, L., and Beck, S. (1966). *Mastering the art of French cooking*. Vol. 1. New York: Knopf.

Cook, J. M. (1963). Italy: Myths and truths. In R. Steele (Ed.), *Italy*. (pp. 31–37). New York: Wilson.

Crossette, B. (2000, November 26). Burgers are the globe's fast food? Not so fast. *The New York Times*, section 4, 2.

Larsen, D. M., et al. (1993). The effects of flour type and dough retardation time on sensory characteristics of pizza crust. *Cereal Chemistry 70*, 647–50.

A meal that's easy as pie: How to pick a pizza that's good and healthful. (1997, January) *Consumer Reports 62*, 19–23.

Pizza. (1997). In *The new encyclopaedia Britannica* (Vol. 9, p. 490). Chicago: Encyclopaedia Britannica.

Schrambling, R. (1988, February). Tex-Mex pizza. *Working Woman*, 125.

U.S. Department of Agriculture. (1990, March). Calories and weight: The USDA pocket guide. *DietSearch: News and articles*. Retrieved January 10, 2001 from http:www.dietsearch.com/article/calories/htm

DOCUMENTATION: THE CHICAGO STYLE (FOOTNOTES)

This traditional system is the best choice for a report for a general audience; for courses in art, business, communications, dance, journalism, law, music, theater, history, or political science; and for cross-disciplinary courses.

With footnotes, you place a raised numeral in your paper every time you present information from your research—either at the end of the summary, paraphrase, or quotation (after the quotation marks), or within the sentence, right after the fact or statistic. The raised numeral is then repeated at the bottom of that page (see the example below), with the specific source of the information.

The numbers for this footnoting system are continuous; that is, you begin with the number *one* and progress, using the next number each time you document a fact or quotation from your research. Thus, one source may be referred to several times, but each new use of material from that source will have a new number. After the first complete footnote, subsequent footnotes for that source give only the last name of the author and the appropriate page number.

The advantages of this system are that

- If readers are curious about the source, they can easily glance down to the bottom of the page.

- The writer of the paper can make interpretive or explanatory comments.[1]

Computers simplify this system of presenting sources. In most word processing programs, you can indicate where you want the number to be inserted, specify whether you want a footnote or endnote, and then type the content of each note as you go through the documentation of your paper. The computer will automatically format the notes and will keep track of your sequence of numbers both during composition and revision.

---

1. The footnote can add a comment that would otherwise clutter up your paper.

■ FORMAT FOR FOOTNOTES

If your word processing program does not format footnotes automatically, follow these guidelines:

- Footnotes begin at the bottom of the page—four lines below the last line of text—and correspond to the numbers given in the text on that page.

- First draw a two-inch line (twelve strokes of the underline key) and skip a line.

- Indent five spaces and give the appropriate numeral, followed by a period and a space. Subsequent lines within each entry begin at the left margin.

For Books

- Give the name of the author, first name first, followed by a comma and a space.

- Give the title, italicized, followed by a space. Give the name of an editor or a number for the edition, if necessary, after a comma; otherwise use no punctuation.

- After an opening parenthesis, give first the city of publication, followed by a colon and one space.

- Then give the name of the publisher, followed by a comma and one space.

- Give the date of copyright, then a closing parenthesis, followed by a comma, then a space.

- Give the page number(s), without p. or pp. End the entry with a period.

    2. Louise Love, *The Complete Book of Pizza* (Evanston, IL: Sassafras, 1980), 35.

For Articles

- Give the name of the author, if given, first name first, followed by a comma and a space.

- Give the title of the article in quotation marks, with a comma inside the closing quotation marks.

- After one space, give the title of the periodical, italicized and followed by no punctuation.

- Give the volume number for scholarly journals and enclose the date in parentheses, followed by a comma.

  3. "Cooking School: Pizza," *The Magazine of La Cucina Italiana* 5 (July/August 2000), 102.

- Give the date of a nonscholarly periodical—day, month, and year with no punctuation and one space between—in parentheses and followed by a colon and one space.

  4. Amy Scherber, "Pizza with a 'Push Button' Crust," *New York Times* (15 September 1999): F5.

- Give the page number(s) followed by a period.

For Websites

- Give the name of the author, first name first, followed by a period and a space. If no author is listed, give the name of the sponsoring organization if known.

- Give the title of the article if it is part of a larger website. Use quotation marks with a comma inside the closing quotation marks.

- Give the title of the website, italicized.

- In square brackets, write *cited* followed by the date you viewed it [cited June 4, 2001]. Add a period.

- Write *Available from the World Wide Web,* followed by the address of the website, in angle brackets. End the entry with a period.

  5. U.S. Department of Agriculture. "Calories and Weight: The USDA Pocket Guide," *DietSearch: News and Articles.* March 1990 [cited 1 Jan. 2000]. Available from the World Wide Web: <http:www.dietsearch.com/article/calories/htm>.

CHICAGO

Here is an example of a paragraph using footnotes. Check the numerals and the matching footnotes at the bottom of the page:

When the first pizzeria opened in New York City in 1905, it introduced the classic Italian pizza--bread dough covered with tomato sauce and cheese.[1] Now, almost a century later, the simple pizza has been transformed into an American creation that reflects this country's love of diversity. In addition to the classic version, pizza lovers can now savor just about every combination and concoction imaginable. The National Association of Pizza Operators reports that "Pizza makers have tried virtually every type of food on pizzas, including peanut butter and jelly, bacon and eggs, and mashed potatoes."[2] Gourmet versions, such as the Tex-Mex, which Regina Schrambling says is "welcomed by most Americans," continue to satisfy our taste for the unusual.[3] From France comes the pissaladière, which adds fresh herbs, black olives, and anchovies.[4] Even America's exports reflect our adaptability; for example, Domino's

---

1. *Encyclopaedia Britannica: Micropaedia.* 1997 ed. s.v. "Pizza."
2. Quoted in "A Meal That's Easy as Pie: How to Pick a Pizza That's Good and Healthful." *Consumer Reports* (January 1997): 19–23.
3. Regina Schrambling, "Tex-Mex Pizza." *Working Woman* (February 1988): 125.
4. Julia Child, Louisette Bertholle, and Simone Beck, *Mastering the Art of French Cooking,* vol. 1. (New York: Knopf, 1966), 151.

uses pickled ginger and chicken on its pizzas in India.[5] You might have to travel to Italy to get real Italian pizza; but you can eat your way across this country--and the world-- sampling several hundred modern versions of pizza made the American way.

■ A VARIATION: ENDNOTES

This system is the same as the footnote system, except the footnotes are moved from the foot of each page and are instead accumulated in numerical order at the end of the paper on a separate page, called *Notes*.

Format for Endnotes

- After the title, *Notes* (centered), skip two lines and indent the first line five spaces.

- Give the numeral followed by a period.

- Skip a space and then begin the note.

- Use the same format as for footnotes.

- Double-space the entire page.

Like footnotes, endnotes require a Bibliography.

Bibliography

The *Bibliography,* at the end of the paper, is a list of all the sources referred to in the footnotes. Each source is listed only once—in alphabetical order by the authors' last names (not in the order you used them), and in the same format as for the footnotes, with these exceptions:

- Do not number the list.

- Double-space the entire list and do not add extra spaces between entries.

---

5. Barbara Crossette, "Burgers Are the Globe's Fast Food? Not So Fast." New York Times, 26 November 2000, sec. 4:2.

- Use reverse indentation, beginning each entry at the left margin and indenting subsequent lines five spaces or half an inch.

- Reverse the authors' names, last name first. Reverse only the names of the first author listed when there are co-authors.

- Follow the author's name with a period.

- For articles, follow the title with a period (inside the quotation marks).

- For books, newspapers, and popular magazines, omit parentheses around dates and other publishing information.

- For journal articles, place the date in parentheses after the volume number—just as in footnotes.

In addition, this system allows you to list a *Supplementary Bibliography*—a list of sources that you read for background or tangential information but did not actually refer to in the report.

CHICAGO

Bibliography

Child, Julia, Louisette Bertholle, and Simone
Beck. *Mastering the Art of French Cooking.*
2 vols. New York: Knopf, 1966.

Crossette, Barbara. "Burgers Are the Globe's
Fast Food? Not So Fast." *New York Times,*
26 November 2000, sec. 4: 2.

Encyclopaedia Britannica: Micropaedia. 1997 ed.
s.v. "Pizza."

"A Meal That's Easy as Pie: How to Pick a Pizza
That's Good and Healthful." *Consumer Reports*
January 1997: 19–23.

Schrambling, Regina. "Tex-Mex Pizza." *Working
Woman* February 1988: 125.

U.S. Department of Agriculture. "Calories and
Weight: The USDA Pocket Guide," *DietSearch:
News and Articles.* March 1990. [Cited 10
January 2001]. Available from the World Wide
Web <http:www.dietsearch.com/
article/calories/htm>.

PART 4

GROWING AS A WRITER

Keeping a Journal

Keeping a journal is one of the best ways to grow as a writer. A journal helps you put your thoughts and feelings into words, helps you overcome writer's block, and helps you develop your own personal style. You will also discover truths you didn't know—about yourself and about many topics. Some of your journal writing can later be developed into complete essays or stories.

A journal is different from a diary (a day-by-day list of what you do). A journal can include memories, feelings, observations, hopes. It gives you the opportunity to try your hand at different types of writing, so aim for variety in your entries.

Some Guidelines for Keeping a Journal

- Write several times a week for at least ten minutes.

- Write in ink. Date each entry.

- If you have no topic, write whatever comes into your head or choose one of the suggestions from the list given here.

- While you write, don't worry about correctness. Write as spontaneously and as honestly as you can, and let your thoughts and words flow freely.

- At your leisure, reread your entries and make any corrections or additions you like. Remember, this journal is for *you*, and it will be a source of delight to you in years to come.

Some Suggestions for Journal Entries

Blow off steam.

Describe someone you love.

Tell your favorite story about yourself when you were little.

State a controversial opinion and then defend your position.

Respond to a movie, a TV program, a book, an article, a concert, a song.

Write a letter to someone and say what you can't say face to face.

Describe in full detail a place you know and love.

Remember on paper your very first boyfriend or girlfriend.

Relate, using present tense, a memorable dream you've had.

Sit in front of a drawing or painting and write down the feelings and images it evokes in you.

Analyze the personal trait that gets you in trouble most often.

Relate an incident in which you were proud (or ashamed) of yourself.

Describe your dream house.

Capture on paper some object—such as a toy or article of clothing—that you loved as a child or love now.

Go all the way back: Try to remember your very first experience in the world and describe how it looked to you then.

Write down a family story. Include when and where you have heard it.

Choose something you'd like to know more about—or need to know more about—and tell why.

Set down a "here and now" scene: Record sensory details right at the moment you're experiencing them.

Go to a public place and observe people. Write down your observations.

Explain your most pressing problem at present.

Analyze your relationship to food.

Explain exactly how to do some activity you know well. Use sketches if you need to illustrate or clarify your point.

Write about yourself as a writer.

Trace the history of your hair.

Take one item from today's newspaper and give your thoughts about it.

Commit yourself in writing to doing something you've always wanted to do but never have.

Adding Details

Details give life to your ideas. As you write, you naturally concentrate on your ideas, but the reader will best remember a strong example or fact.

Adding Information

If a teacher asks for "more details," you probably have written a generalization with insufficient support. You need to slow down, take *one* idea at a time, and tell what it is based upon. You cannot assume that the reader agrees with you or knows what you're talking about. You have to say where you got your idea. This comes down to adding some of the following details to support your point:

- Examples
- Facts
- Logical reasoning
- Explanation of abstract words

Ideas are abstract and hard to picture. To be remembered, they must be embodied in concrete language—in pictures, in facts, in things that happened.

For example, here are three abstract statements:

> Gloria means what she says.
> The scene in the film was romantic.
> The paramecium displayed peculiar behavior.

Now here they are made more concrete:

> Gloria means what she says. She says she hates television, and she backs it up by refusing to date any man who watches TV.

> The soft focus of the camera and the violin music in the background heightened the romance of the scene.

> Under the microscope, the paramecium displayed peculiar behavior. It doubled in size and turned purple.

Adding Sensory Details

The best writing appeals to our five senses. Your job as a writer is to put down words that will cause the reader to see, hear, smell, taste, or feel exactly what you experienced.

You can sharpen your senses with "here and now" exercises.

- Observe and write exactly what you see, feel, smell, taste, and hear moment by moment. Expand your descriptions until they become very specific.

- Write a paragraph describing a memory you have of a smell, a taste, a sight, a sound, a feeling (either a touch or a sensation).

- Take one object—an orange, a frying pan, a leaf—and describe it completely, using as many sensory details as possible.

These exercises will help build the habit of including careful observation in your writing.

Adding Word Power

Never underestimate the power of one good word. It's worth taking a look at each word in your sentence or paragraph to evaluate whether that word represents your best effort.

Choose words that are

- Concrete rather than abstract

- Short rather than long

- Simple rather than complex

- Informative rather than impressive

- Personal rather than impersonal

Don't just pull a word out of a thesaurus. Instead, choose words that are familiar to you and that say exactly what you mean.

Recognizing Clichés

A cliché is a *predictable* word, phrase, or statement. If it sounds very familiar, if it comes very easily, it's probably a cliché. Clichés are comfortable, and they are usually true. In conversation, clichés are often acceptable, but in writing they can either annoy or bore the reader. Learn to recognize clichés and replace them with fresher, sharper language.

Recognize Clichés

Some clichés are old sayings; others are expressions that are either worn out or trendy.

Nobody's perfect	Like a beached whale
Crying over spilt milk	Madly in love
Slept like a log	Easier said than done
Smooth as silk	User-friendly
By leaps and bounds	Cool
Wining and dining	

This year's new expression is next year's cliché. (Try saying "groovy" to your friends.)

Eliminate Clichés

- Often you can simply omit a cliché—you don't need it. The essay is better without it.

- At other times, replace the cliché by saying what you mean. Give the details.

- Look out for clichés in your conclusion; that's where they love to gather.

- Make up your own comparisons and descriptions. Have fun being creative.

You might start by rewriting some of the clichés in this chapter.

Eliminating Offensive Language

Offensive language includes slang, vulgarity, and all expressions that demean or exclude people. To avoid offending your reader, examine both the words you use and their underlying assumptions.

Offensive Word Choices

Some wording is prejudiced or impolite or outdated:

Eliminate name-calling, slurs, or derogatory nicknames. Instead, refer to groups by the names they use for themselves. For example, use *African Americans* (not *colored people*), *Asian* (not *Oriental*). If you criticize a group, explain your position rather than tossing in a nasty phrase.

Replace words using *man* or the *-ess* ending with nonsexist terms. For example, use *flight attendant* (not *stewardess*), *mechanic* (not *repairman*), *leader* or *diplomat* (not *statesman*).

False Assumptions

Some statements are based on hidden biases. Look hard at references to any group—even one you belong to.

Check for stereotyping about innate abilities or flaws in members of a group. For example, all women are not maternal, all lawyers are not devious, all Southerners are not racist, and all Japanese are not industrious. Many clichés are based in stereotypes: *absent-minded professor, dumb jock, Latin temper.*

Check assumptions that certain jobs are best filled by certain ethnic groups or one sex. For example, all nurses aren't women; all mechanics aren't men; all ballet dancers aren't Russian.

Watch for inconsistency. The following list assumes that everyone is a white man unless otherwise specified:

> two Republicans, a Democrat, an Independent, a woman, and an African American

Instead, use

> three Republicans, two Democrats, and an Independent

Faulty Pronoun Usage

Check Pronouns for bias:

> Each Supreme Court justice should have *his clerk* attend the conference.

- One option for revision is to use *his* or *her.*

> Each Supreme Court justice should have *his* or *her* clerk attend the conference.

- A better solution is to use the plural throughout.

> The Supreme Court justices should have *their* clerks attend the conference.

- Often the most graceful solution is to eliminate the pronoun.

> Each Supreme Court justice should have a clerk attend the conference.

You can find more help with pronoun choice in the section "Consistent Pronouns," (pages 18–20).

Trimming Wordiness

Often we think that people are impressed by a writer who uses big words and long sentences. Actually, people are more impressed by a writer who is *clear.*

Cut Empty Words

Some words sound good but carry no clear meaning. Omitting them will often make the sentence sharper.

experience	proceeded to
situation	the fact that
is a man who	really
personality	thing
in today's society	something

In the following examples, the first version is wordy; the second version is trim.

> The fire was a terrifying situation and a depressing experience for all of us.
> The fire terrified and depressed all of us.

> Carmen is a woman who has a tempestuous personality.
> Carmen is tempestuous.

> The reason she quit was because of the fact that she was sick.
> She quit because of illness.

> Anger is something we all feel.
> We all feel anger.

Avoid Redundancy—Pointless Repetition

> He married his wife twelve years ago.
> He married twelve years ago.

> She wore a scarf that was pink in color.
> She wore a pink scarf.

Be Direct

Tell what something *is,* rather than what it *isn't.*

> Captain Bligh was not a very nice man.
> Captain Bligh was vicious.

Replace Fancy or Technical Words

You can replace *utilize* with *use* and *coronary thrombosis* with *heart attack* and bring your paper down to earth. Some subjects may require technical language, but in general, strive to use everyday words.

When you trim, don't worry that your papers will be too short: For length, add examples and further thoughts. Look at the topic from a different viewpoint. Add points, not just words.

Using Strong Verbs

One of the quickest ways to add excitement and forcefulness to your writing is to replace limp verbs with strong ones. Three simple guidelines can help you to do so:

- Replace passive verbs with active verbs.
- Get rid of being verbs.
- Choose dynamic verbs.

Replace Passive Verbs with Active Verbs

You can write a verb in *active voice* or *passive voice:*

> *Passive:* An inspiring talk was given by the president of the college.
> *Active:* The president of the college gave an inspiring talk.

> *Passive:* Several safety precautions should be taken before attempting rock climbing.
> *Active:* Rock climbers should take several safety precautions.

People often use passive verbs when they do not want to name the person who did the action. The passive construction is less direct and therefore less revealing:

> A pedestrian was struck down at the intersection.

> The position of marketing director has been eliminated as of July 1.

> Some mistakes were made by the building committee.

More often than not, you can put energy into your writing by converting passive verbs into active ones.

Get Rid of *Being* Verbs

Being verbs, like *is* and *are,* sap the energy from your writing. The verb *to be* comes in eight forms:

> *am, is, are, was, were, be, being, been*

Often you can replace being verbs with forceful verbs. Go through your writing, circle every form of *be,* and then do your best to replace each one with a dynamic verb—a verb that communicates specific action or creates a picture.

> The audience was irate. People were jumping out of their seats and were coming into the aisles.

This example has three *being* forms. Eliminating the three *being* verbs makes the sentence tighter and more dynamic:

> The irate audience jumped out of their seats and flooded the aisles.

Watch out especially for *there is, there are, there was, there were, it is, it was.* You can usually eliminate these empty constructions:

> It is depressing to watch the national news.
> Watching the national news depresses me.

> There are three people who influenced my choice of career.
> Three people influenced my choice of career.

Save *being* verbs for times when you actually mean a state of being:

> I am totally exhausted.

> She was born on Bastille Day.

Choose Dynamic Verbs

Verbs, because they show action, are usually the strongest words in a sentence, the words that give life to your writing. Keep an eye out for verbs that make a picture:

> The governor circled through the crowd, smiling his painted smile.

> To arrest their attention, I hobbled across the yard and flung myself on the ground.

> Hedy Lamarr lounged her way through life.

> The whole team came roaring down on the umpire when he stumbled over second base and tripped the base runner.

Varying Your Sentences

The same idea can be put in many different ways, and every sentence has movable parts. To get more music or drama into your style, try reading your writing aloud. When you come across choppy or monotonous sentences, use some of the following techniques.

Write an Important Sentence Several Ways

You can turn a sentence that troubles you into a sentence that pleases you. Instead of fiddling with a word here and a word there, try writing five completely different sentences—each with the same idea. One could be long, one short, one a generalization, one a picture, and so forth. Often you'll find that your first isn't your best. If you play with several possibilities, you'll come up with the one you want. This technique works especially well for improving introductions and conclusions.

Use Short Sentences Frequently

Short sentences are the meat and bones of good writing.

- They can simplify an idea.
- They can dramatize a point.
- They can create suspense.
- They can add rhythm.
- They can be blunt and forceful.

If you're getting tangled in too many words, a few short sentences will often get you through.

Remember, however, that you must use a period even between very short but complete sentences:

> It was a rainy Monday. I was sitting at my desk. I heard a knock at the door. I waited. The doorknob turned.

Lengthen Choppy Sentences

Using *only* short sentences can make your writing monotonous. If you want to lengthen a sentence, the simplest way is to add concrete information.

> The book was boring.

> The author's long descriptions of rooms in which nothing and no one ever moved made the book boring.

Combine Choppy Sentences

Combine two short sentences back to back. Here are three ways:

- Put a semicolon between them.

    > Kitty expected Anna Karenina to wear a lavender dress to the ball; Anna chose black.

    (Be sure each half is a complete sentence.)

- Put a comma followed by one of these connectors:

    | but | and | for |
    | or | so | yet |
    | nor | | |

    > Kitty expected Anna Karenina to wear a lavender dress to the ball, but Anna chose black.

- Put a semicolon followed by a transition word and a comma. Here are the most common transition words.

    | however | for example | meanwhile |
    | therefore | furthermore | nevertheless |
    | instead | in other words | on the other hand |
    | besides | | |

    > Kitty expected Anna Karenina to wear a lavender dress to the ball; instead, Anna chose black.

Combine sentences to highlight the major point. Often sentences contain two or more facts. You can show the relationship between these facts so that the most important one stands out.

In the examples below, the first sentence of each pair gives two ideas equal weight. Then the sentence is rewritten to emphasize one idea.

> Martha Grimes was a college professor. She became a best-selling mystery writer.
> Before she became a best-selling mystery writer, Martha Grimes was a college professor.

> I love Earl. He barks at the slightest sound.
> I love Earl even though he barks at the slightest sound.

> Brad lost a contact lens. He had one blue eye and one brown eye.
> Because Brad lost a contact lens, he had one blue eye and one brown eye.

Notice that the halves of the revised sentences can be reversed.

> Although Earl barks at the slightest sound, I still love him.

Usually the sentence gains strength when the most interesting point comes last.

Insert the gist of one sentence inside another:

> Sheila Baldwin makes a fine living as a photographer. She has a great eye for unusual pictures. She is very adventuresome.

> Sheila Baldwin, with her great eye for unusual pictures and her spirit of adventure, makes a fine living as a photographer.

The problem with most choppy sentences is that one after another starts with the subject of the sentence—in this case, *Sheila* or *she*. Sometimes you can use *who* (for people) or *which* (for things) to start an insertion. Sometimes you can reduce the insertion to a word or two.

> I interviewed Nell Partin, who is the mayor, about the sanitation strike.

> I interviewed Nell Partin, the mayor, about the sanitation strike.

Give Your Sentences a Strong Ending

The beginning is worth sixty cents, what's in the middle is worth forty cents, but the end is worth a dollar.

> I walked into the room, looked around at all the flowers my friends had sent, took a deep breath, and collapsed onto the sofa in tears.

> When the nights grow cool and foggy and the full moon rises after the day's harvest, Madeline, so the story goes, roams the hills in search of revenge.

> What Louie Gallagher received, after all the plea-bargaining and haggling and postponements and hearings, was a ten-year sentence.

To stress the most important parts of your sentence, tuck in interrupters or insertions. Put transitions or minor information into the middle of your sentence.

> He argues, as you probably know, even with statues.

> From my point of view, however, that's a mistake.

> The interior decoration, designed by his cousin, looked gaudy.

Remember to put commas on *both* sides of the insertion.

Use Parallel Structure

Parallel structure—repeating certain words for clarity and emphasis—makes elegant sentences.

> To be honest is not necessarily to be brutal.

Famous quotations are often based on parallel structure.

> I came, I saw, I conquered.
>
> —Julius Caesar

> To believe your own thought, to believe that what is true for you in your private heart is true for all men—that is genius.
>
> —Ralph Waldo Emerson

> Ask not what your country can do for you; ask what you can do for your country.
>
> —John F. Kennedy

For the correct usage of parallel structure, see page 50.

Imitate Good Writers

Take a close look at the writings of some of your favorite authors. A good exercise is to pick out a sentence or a paragraph that you particularly like. Read it aloud once or twice; then copy it over several times to get the feel of the language. Now study it closely and try to write an imitation of it. Use the sentence or paragraph as a model, but think up your own ideas and words. This exercise can rapidly expand your power to vary your sentences.

FINDING YOUR VOICE

Often we write the way we think we're supposed to, with big words and fancy sentences. The writing comes out awkward and impersonal. But good writing has the feel of a real person talking.

To find your own voice as a writer, keep these questions in mind when you write:

Am I saying this in plain English?

Are these words that I normally use?

Am I saying what I know to be true instead of what I think others want to hear?

A great technique for developing your own voice is to read your work aloud. If you do it regularly, you'll begin to notice when other voices are intruding or when you are using roundabout phrases. In time, your sentences will gain rhythm and force. Reading aloud helps you to remember that, when you write, you are telling something to somebody. In fact, another good technique is to visualize a particular person and pretend you are writing directly to that person.

Good writing is *honest*. Honest writing requires you to break through your fears of what other people might think of you and to tell what you know to be true.

Postscript

You do your best work when you take pleasure in a job. You write best when you know something about the topic and know what you want to stress. So, when you can, write about a topic you've lived with and have considered over time. When you *have* to write about a topic that seems boring or difficult, get to know it for a while, until it makes sense to you. Start with what is clear to you and you will write well.

Don't quit too soon. Sometimes a few more changes, a little extra attention to fine points, a new paragraph written on a separate piece of paper will transform an acceptable essay into an essay that really pleases you. Through the time you spend writing and rewriting, you will discover what is most important to say.

■ An Invitation

Rules of Thumb was written for you, so we welcome your comments about it and about *Good Measures: A Practice Book to Accompany Rules of Thumb, Rules of Thumb for Research, Rules of Thumb for Business Writers,* and *Rules of Thumb for Online Research.* Please write directly to us:

Jay Silverman
Elaine Hughes
Diana Roberts Wienbroer

Department of English
Nassau Community College
Garden City, New York 11530-6793

If you would like to purchase individual copies of *Rules of Thumb* directly from McGraw-Hill, please call this toll-free number:

1-800-822-8158

For textbook orders and examination copies, call:

1-800-338-3987

Visit McGraw-Hill's Higher Education Website at <www.mhhe.com>.

A List of Valuable Sources

Internet addresses listed here are regularly updated on McGraw-Hill's Website:

http://www.mhhe.com/writers

The following lists include the most basic resources. You'll find these reference materials in one or more of the following formats: *print, microfilm,* or *electronic.* Whenever possible, begin your search with the computer because it is comprehensive and takes less time to use. The sources given here may be listed in a menu of choices on your library's home page, or they may be installed in designated computers, or you may be able to access them directly from home. If you do not find an electronic version, ask the librarian for the print or film version.

INDEXES

Bibliographic Index: A Cumulative Bibliography of Bibliographies

Business Index

ERIC
(educational resources)   http://ericir.syr.edu

Humanities Citation Index

Humanities Index

Infoline

InfoTrac

Magazine Index

Medline   http://www.ncbi.nlm.nih.gov/PubMed

http://www.healthgate.com

MLA(Modern Language Association) International Bibliography (for literature)

New York Times Index

Periodicals Index

Reader's Guide to Periodical Literature

Science Citation Index

Science Index

Social Science Citation Index

Social Science Index

Westlaw

MULTISEARCH DATABASES

ABI-Inform

FirstSearch

Lexis-Nexis

STATISTICAL SOURCES

American Statistical Index (also on CD-ROM.; see also individual federal agencies' websites)

http://www.fedstats.gov

Bureau of Census Reports (various reports; some are on CD-ROM)

http://www.census.gov

Statistical Resources on the Web

http://www.lib.umich.edu/libhome/Documents.center/stats.html

SUBJECT DIRECTORIES

About.com (each area is maintained by an expert to whom you can e-mail)

http://www.about.com

Magellan (good subject search)	http://magellan.excite.com
Yahoo (very fast subject search of a huge database)	http://www.yahoo.com

GENERAL AND LIBRARY REFERENCE PAGES

CMC Information Services (lists search engines and links to a variety of resources)	http://www/december.com/cmc/info
E-Server at University of Washington (links to many free electronic texts)	http://eserver.org
Librarians' Index to the Internet	http://sunsite.berkeley.edu/InternetIndex
Library of Congress Research Tools	http://lcweb.loc.gov/rr/tools.html
Literary Resources on the Web	http://andromeda.rutgers.edu/~jlynch/Lit
My Virtual Reference Desk	http://www.refdesk.com
World Lecture Hall (faculty websites, organized by discipline)	http://www.utexas.edu/world/lecture

SEARCH ENGINES

AltaVista (one of the most comprehensive)	http://altavista.com
Dogpile (fun to use, it simultaneously searches twenty-five search engines)	http://www.dogpile.com
FastSearch (fast)	http://www.fastsearch.com
Google (huge database, retrieves at a high relevance)	http://www.google.com

Highway 61 (very fast, it searches the six most popular search engines and arranges the results by relevance)

http://www.highway61.com

NorthernLight (one of the most thorough of the search engines)

http://www.northernlight.com

ASK AN EXPERT

Ask an Expert Sources

http://www.cln.org/int_expert.html

Ask Jeeves

http://www.ask.com

Scientific American Ask the Experts

http://www.sciam.com/askexpert/index.html

JOURNALS AND NEWS SOURCES ONLINE

Christian Science Monitor (complete issues since 1980)

http://www.csmonitor.com

National Public Radio

http://www.npr.org

Newspaper Archives

http://metalab.unc.edu/slanews/internet/archives.html

New York Times (also on microfilm, complete since 1851)

http://www.nytimes.com

Online Magazines

http://www.pathfinder.com

Public Broadcasting System

http://www.pbs.org

Selected Electronic Journals

http://www.library.uiuc.edu/edx/uiucejrn.htm

University of Houston Library: Scholarly Journals Distributed through the World Wide Web

http://info.lib.uh.edu/wj/letters.htm

HELP WITH STYLE, GRAMMAR, AND USAGE

Ammer, Christine. *American Heritage Dictionary of Idioms.*
Boston: Houghton, 1997. An explanation of the meaning of
phrases and when to use which preposition in a phrase
(especially helpful for ESL).

Burchfield, R. W., ed. *The New Fowler's English Usage.* 3rd ed.
New York: Oxford, 2000. A thorough coverage of word
usage.

Jack Lynch's page (grammar and style notes)	http://andromeda.rutgers. edu/~jlynch/writing

Merriam Webster's Collegiate Dictionary. 10th ed. Boston:
Merriam-Webster, 1998. Also at <http://www.m-w.com>.

OWL (Online Writing Lab at Purdue University)	http://www/owl.trc. purdue.edu/prose.html
Punctuation Miscellany	http://www.fas.harvard. edu/~wricntr/comma.html
University of Maine's Links to other Writing Centers	http://www.ume.maine.edu/ ~wcenter/others.html
Web of Online Dictionaries	http://www.facstaf.bucknell. edu/rbeard/diction.html

HELP WITH FORMAT FOR RESEARCH PAPERS

American Psychological Association. *1994 Publication Manual of
the American Psychological Association.* Washington, DC:
American Psychological Association, 1994. Also see the
APA website <http://www.APA.org>.

Gibaldi, Joseph. *MLA Handbook for Writers of Research Papers.*
5th ed. New York: Modern Language Association, 1999.
Also see the MLA website <http://www.mla.org>.

University of Chicago Press. *The Chicago Manual of Style.*
14th ed. Chicago: U of Chicago P, 1993. Also see their website
<http://www.press.uchicago.edu/Misc/Chicago/cmosfaq
.html>.

About the Authors

A graduate of Amherst College and the University of Virginia, **Jay Silverman** has received fellowships from the Fulbright-Hayes Foundation, the Andrew Mellon Foundation, and the National Endowment for the Humanities. Dr. Silverman has taught at Virginia Highlands Community College and at Nassau Community College where he received the Honors Program award for Excellence in Teaching and where he also teaches in the College Bound Program of the Nassau County Mental Health Association.

Elaine Hughes moved to New York City from Mississippi in 1979 to attend a National Endowment for the Humanities seminar at Columbia University. She taught writing for more than twenty-five years, primarily at Hinds Community College in Raymond, Mississippi, and at Nassau Community College. After her retirement from NCC and her return to Mississippi, she conducted many writing workshops for the Esalen Institute and for other organizations. Recently she won a Mississippi Arts Council grant for creative nonfiction. She is also the author of *Writing from the Inner Self.* Just before the publication of this book, Elaine Hughes passed away after more than 20 years of victories over breast cancer.

As Chair of the English Department of Nassau Community College for six years, **Diana Roberts Wienbroer** coordinated a department of 150 faculty members and served on the Executive Council of the Association of Departments of English. Besides teaching writing for over thirty years, both in Texas and New York, she has studied and taught film criticism. She is also the author of *Rules of Thumb for Online Research.* Since her retirement from NCC, she has taught seminars on Internet research and effective business writing.

The authors have also written *Rules of Thumb for Research, Rules of Thumb for Business Writers,* and *Good Measures: A Practice Book to Accompany Rules of Thumb,* all available from McGraw-Hill.

Numbers in **boldface** indicate the main coverage of a topic that is presented in several places.

TroubleShooting Guide

Problems with Correctness and Style

Punctuation

Start with pages 28–33 (comma vs. period—run-on sentences, comma splices, sentence fragments).
See pages 34–35 for comma rules.
See pages 36–39 for semicolons, colons, dashes, and parentheses.

Apostrophes, see page 17.

Quotation marks, see pages 40–43.

Titles, see page 44.

Spelling

Start with pages 3–7 (the most commonly confused words).
For the basic spelling rules, see pages 10–12.
For common misspellings, study the examples on pages 10–12.

Pronoun errors

Singulars and plurals, see pages 18–20.
I vs. *me*, see pages 21–22.

Verb errors

Agreement of subject and verb, see page 47.
Mixed verb tenses, see pages 45–46.
Passive verbs, see pages 158–59.

Word endings

Start with pages 48–49.
Also study pages 10, 17, and 47.

Parallel structure, see pages 50 and 163.

Dangling constructions, see page 51.

Awkward writing

Start with pages 156–57 and 165.
Study pages 23–24 and 50–52.

Sentence variety, see pages 160–64.